Lecture Notes in Computer Science 15421

W0235399

The series Lecture Notes in Computer Science (LNCS), including its subseries Lecture Notes in Artificial Intelligence (LNAI) and Lecture Notes in Bioinformatics (LNBI), has established itself as a medium for the publication of new developments in computer science and information technology research, teaching, and education.

LNCS enjoys close cooperation with the computer science R & D community, the series counts many renowned academics among its volume editors and paper authors, and collaborates with prestigious societies. Its mission is to serve this international community by providing an invaluable service, mainly focused on the publication of conference and workshop proceedings and postproceedings. LNCS commenced publication in 1973.

Xiuqin Pan · Mengxing Huang · Jiajia Zhang ·
Junyang Chen · Liang-Jie Zhang
Editors

AI and Multimodal Services – AIMS 2024

13th International Conference
Held as Part of the Services Conference Federation, SCF 2024
Bangkok, Thailand, November 16–19, 2024
Proceedings

 Springer

Editors
Xiuqin Pan
Minzu University of China
Beijing, China

Mengxing Huang
Hainan University
Haikou, China

Jiajia Zhang
Harbin Institute of Technology
Harbin, China

Junyang Chen
Shenzhen University
Shenzhen, China

Liang-Jie Zhang 🄳
Shenzhen University
Shenzhen, China

ISSN 0302-9743   ISSN 1611-3349 (electronic)
Lecture Notes in Computer Science
ISBN 978-3-031-77680-9   ISBN 978-3-031-77681-6 (eBook)
https://doi.org/10.1007/978-3-031-77681-6

Preface

The 2024 International Conference on AI and Multimodal Services (AIMS 2024) was the emerging theme-topic conference for the development, publication, discovery, orchestration, invocation, testing, delivery, certification, and management of artificial intelligence (AI) and multimodal applications and services. Part of SCF 2018, AIMS 2018 was successfully held on June 25 – June 30, 2018, in Seattle, USA. Part of SCF 2019, AIMS 2019 was successfully held on June 25–30, 2019, in San Diego, USA. Part of SCF 2020 and SCF 2021, AIMS 2020 and AIMS 2021 were successfully held over the Internet. AIMS 2022 was successfully held on December 10–14, 2022, in Honolulu, Hawaii, USA. AIMS 2023 was successfully held on September 23–26, 2023, in Honolulu, Hawaii, USA. In 2024, we celebrated our 2024 version of the gathering, to strive to advance the largest international professional forum on AI and multimodal services.

AIMS 2024 was a member of Services Conference Federation (SCF). SCF 2024 had the following 10 collocated service-oriented sister conferences: 2024 International Conference on Web Services (ICWS 2024), 2024 International Conference on Cloud Computing (CLOUD 2024), 2024 International Conference on Services Computing (SCC 2024), 2024 International Conference on Big Data (BigData 2024), 2024 International Conference on AI and Multimodal Services (AIMS 2024), 2024 International Conference on Metaverse (METAVERSE 2024), 2024 International Conference on Internet of Things (ICIOT 2024), 2024 International Conference on Cognitive Computing (ICCC 2024), 2024 International Conference on Edge Computing (EDGE 2024), and 2024 International Conference on Blockchain (ICBC 2024).

This volume presents the accepted papers of the 2024 International Conference on AI and Multimodal Services (AIMS 2024), held in Bangkok, Thailand during November 16–19, 2024. For this conference, each paper was single-blind reviewed by three independent members of the International Program Committee. After carefully evaluating their originality and quality, we accepted 8 papers.

We are pleased to thank the authors whose submissions and participation made this conference possible. We also want to express our thanks to the Organizing Committee and Program Committee members, for their dedication in helping to organize the conference and reviewing the submissions. We owe special thanks to the keynote speakers for their impressive speeches.

Finally, we would like to thank operations team members Jing Zeng, Sheng He, Yishuang Ning, and Zhuolin Mei for their excellent work in organizing this conference.

We look forward to your future great contributions as a volunteer, author, and conference participant in the fast-growing worldwide services innovations community.

September 2024

Xiuqin Pan
Mengxing Huang
Jiajia Zhang
Junyang Chen
Liang-Jie Zhang

Organization

Program Chairs

Xiuqin Pan	Minzu University of China, China
Mengxing Huang	Hainan University, China
Jiajia Zhang	Harbin Institute of Technology, China
Junyang Chen (Vice-chair)	Shenzhen University, China

Services Conference Federation (SCF 2024)

General Chairs

Ali Arsanjani	Google, USA
Wu Chou	Essenlix Corporation, USA

Coordinating Program Chair

Liang-Jie Zhang	Shenzhen University, China

CFO and International Affairs Chair

Min Luo	Georgia Tech, USA

Operation Committee

Jing Zeng	China Gridcom Co., Ltd., China
Yishuang Ning	Tsinghua University, China
Sheng He	Kingdee International Software Group Co., Ltd., China
Zhuolin Mei	Jiujiang University, China

Steering Committee

Calton Pu (Co-chair)	Georgia Tech, USA
Liang-Jie Zhang (Co-chair)	Shenzhen University, China

AIMS 2022 Program Committee

Na Sun	Minzu University of China, China
Hong Zhang	Minzu University of China, China
Zhongjian Dai	Beijing Institute of Technology, China
Guangming Li	Dongguan University of Technology, China
Xiaokun Wang	University of Science and Technology Beijing, China
XiuQin Pan	Minzu University of China, China
XiaoYuan Li	Zhengzhou University, China

Conference Sponsor – Services Society

The Services Society (S2) is a non-profit professional organization that has been created to promote worldwide research and technical collaboration in services innovations among academia and industrial professionals. Its members are volunteers from industry and academia with common interests. S2 is registered in the USA as a "501(c) organization", which means that it is an American tax-exempt nonprofit organization. S2 collaborates with other professional organizations to sponsor or co-sponsor conferences and to promote an effective services curriculum in colleges and universities. S2 initiates and promotes a "Services University" program worldwide to bridge the gap between industrial needs and university instruction.

The Services Sector accounted for 79.5% of the GDP of the USA in 2016. The Services Society has formed 5 Special Interest Groups (SIGs) to support technology- and domain-specific professional activities.

- Special Interest Group on Services Computing (SIG-SC)
- Special Interest Group on Big Data (SIG-BD)
- Special Interest Group on Cloud Computing (SIG-CLOUD)
- Special Interest Group on Artificial Intelligence (SIG-AI)
- Special Interest Group on Metaverse (SIG-Metaverse)

About Services Conference Federation (SCF)

As the founding member of the Services Conference Federation (SCF), the first **International Conference on Web Services (ICWS)** was held in June 2003 in Las Vegas, USA. Meanwhile, the First International Conference on Web Services - Europe 2003 (ICWS-Europe 2003) was held in Germany in October 2003. ICWS-Europe 2003 was an extended event of the 2003 International Conference on Web Services (ICWS 2003) in Europe. In 2004, ICWS-Europe was changed to the European Conference on Web Services (ECOWS), which was held at Erfurt, Germany. Sponsored by the Services Society and Springer, SCF 2018 and SCF 2019 were held successfully in Seattle and San Diego, USA. SCF 2020 and SCF 2021 were held successfully online and in Shenzhen, China. SCF 2022 and 2023 were held successfully in Hawaii, USA. To celebrate its 22nd birthday, SCF 2024 was held on November 16–19, 2024, in Bangkok, Thailand.

In the past 21 years, the ICWS community has expanded from Web engineering innovations to scientific research for the whole services industry. Service delivery platforms have been expanded to mobile platforms, Internet of Things, cloud computing, and edge computing. The services ecosystem has gradually been enabled, value added, and intelligence embedded through enabling technologies such as big data, artificial intelligence, and cognitive computing. In the coming years, all transactions with multiple parties involved will be transformed to blockchain.

Based on technology trends and best practices in the field, the Services Conference Federation (SCF) will continue serving as the conference umbrella's code name for all services-related conferences. SCF 2024 defined the future of New ABCDE (AI, Blockchain, Cloud, BigData & IOT) and entered the 5G for Services Era. The theme of ICWS 2024 was Web-based Services for Metaverse Era. We are very proud to announce that SCF 2024's 10 co-located theme topic conferences all centered around "services", with each focusing on exploring different themes (web-based services, cloud-based services, Big Data-based services, services innovation lifecycle, AI-driven ubiquitous services, blockchain-driven trust service ecosystems, industry-specific services and applications, and emerging service-oriented technologies).

- Bigger Platform: The 10 collocated conferences (SCF 2024) were sponsored by the Services Society, which is the world-leading not-for-profit organization (501(c)(3)) dedicated to the service of more than 30,000 worldwide Services Computing researchers and practitioners. A bigger platform means bigger opportunities for all volunteers, authors, and participants. Meanwhile, Springer provided sponsorship of the best paper awards and other professional activities. All the 10 conference proceedings of SCF 2024 were published by Springer and indexed in the ISI Conference Proceedings Citation Index (included in Web of Science), Engineering Index EI (Compendex and Inspec databases), DBLP, Google Scholar, IO-Port, MathSciNet, Scopus, and ZBlMath.
- Brighter Future: While celebrating the 2024 version of ICWS, SCF 2024 highlighted the International Conference on AI and Multimodal Services (AIMS 2024) to build

the fundamental infrastructure for enabling AIGC services ecosystems. It will also lead our community members to create their own brighter future.
- Better Model: SCF 2024 continued to leverage the invented Conference Blockchain Model (CBM) to innovate the organizing practices for all the 10 theme conferences. Senior researchers in the field are welcome to submit proposals to serve as CBM Ambassador for an individual conference to start better interactions during your leadership role in for organizing future SCF conferences.

Contents

Research Track

A Paradigm Shift to Causal Model-Driven Decision-Making With Generative AI

Sheng He[1,2](✉) (iD), Yishuang Ning[1,2], Liang-Jie Zhang[3](iD), and Kai Lei[4](✉) (iD)

[1] National Engineering Research Center for Supporting Software of Enterprise
Internet Services, Shenzhen 518057, China
[2] Kingdee Research, Kingdee International Software Group Co., Ltd., Shenzhen
518057, China
heshengpku@gmail.com
[3] College of Computer Science and Software Engineering, Shenzhen University,
Shenzhen 518060, China
[4] Shenzhen Key Laboratory for Information Centric Networking and Blockchain
Technology (ICNLAB), Peking University, Shenzhen 518055, China
leik@pkusz.edu.cn

Abstract. In recent years, the rise of big data has popularized data-driven decision-making. However, the interpretability shortcomings of artificial intelligence (AI) models limit their reliability for critical decisions. This paper proposes a paradigm shift from conventional data-driven to causal model-driven decision-making, leveraging advancements in causal inference and large language models (LLMs). By applying the capabilities of generative AI, this paradigm shift enables the fusion of extensive domain knowledge, facilitating the development of causal models that capture the complexity of real-world systems and problems. The model-driven approach provides a better understanding of the causal mechanisms, relationships, and dynamics compared to correlational data-driven methods. Moreover, we introduce the concept of a composable business model based on modular causal components. We present a methodology for constructing robust causal model-driven decision frameworks, emphasizing the comprehensive utilization of generative AI to incorporate domain knowledge with causal inferences. Through an in-depth analysis of case studies across multiple domains, this model-driven approach empirically showcases its potential to improve decision quality, optimize resource allocation, and enhance process efficiency. Additionally, we critically discuss future research directions and challenges in the evolutionary trajectory of causal model-driven decision-making.

Keywords: Model-Driven · Decision-Making · Causal Inference · Generative AI · Data-Driven

1 Introduction

In the past decades, the exponential growth of big data has revolutionized decision-making across various domains [1–3]. Organizations now heavily rely on

X. Pan et al. (Eds.): AIMS 2024, LNCS 15421, pp. 3–19, 2025.
https://doi.org/10.1007/978-3-031-77681-6_1

data-driven approaches [4], utilizing statistical analyses of large-scale datasets to inform critical business decisions. However, the increasing complexity of real-world systems demands a deeper and more comprehensive understanding than what traditional data-driven methods can provide.

One of the foremost challenges intrinsic to data-driven decision-making lies in the inherent lack of interpretability associated with these methodologies such as artificial intelligence (AI) [5]. As insights are derived solely from patterns observed in data, without the integration of domain knowledge or intuition [6], the resulting models often lack transparency. This limitation is particularly evident in scenarios where decisions carry significant consequences. The deficiency arises due to the inadequacy of correlation-based insights provided by data-driven techniques, thereby failing to present a precise comprehension of the underlying causal mechanisms and dynamics [7–9].

To overcome these critical limitations, there is an urgent need to transition towards causal model-driven decision-making. This paradigm shift is prompted by recent strides in causal inference methodologies and the applications of large language models (LLMs). Causal inference techniques serve as instrumental tools in fostering the development of robust models capable of encapsulating the complexities inherent in real-world systems. Leveraging the capabilities of LLMs and generative AI introduces a novel dimension, facilitating the seamless integration of extensive domain knowledge into the fabric of causal models.

This integration of generative AI and domain expertise represents a significant advancement, promoting a more powerful comprehension of causal relationships compared to correlational data-driven approaches. The model-driven approach imparts superior insights into the causal mechanisms, relationships, and dynamics, particularly pivotal in high-stakes decision-making scenarios such as healthcare, finance, and public policy. Moreover, the adoption of modular causal components predicated on directed acyclic graphs (DAGs) not only introduces the prospect of composable business models [10] but also augments the adaptability and efficiency of decision-making frameworks.

The main contributions of this paper include the introduction of a novel causal model-driven framework that integrates causal inference techniques with LLMs and generative AI to enhance the depth and accuracy of decision-making processes. The paper is organized as follows. Section 2 critically investigates the imperative and rationale underpinning the transition from data-driven to causal model-driven decision-making, drawing on insights from relevant literature. Section 3 outlines the methodology for integrating generative AI and domain knowledge into the decision-making process, emphasizing the development of composable business models through modular causal components. Section 4 discusses a robust causal model-driven decision-making framework, addressing key components such as data preprocessing, model training, and causal inference techniques. In Sect. 5, real-world applications across diverse domains are examined through case studies, showcasing the effectiveness of the proposed causal model-driven decision-making framework. Finally, Sect. 6 summarizes the key findings and insights of the paper, which also proposes future research directions and challenges of causal model-driven decision-making.

2 Literature Review

In the landscape of decision-making, the widespread adoption of data-driven approaches, facilitated by statistical and machine learning models, has become ubiquitous across various domains. Despite their prevalence, these methods face significant challenges, including a lack of interpretability, sensitivity to spurious correlations, and an intrinsic limitation in establishing causal relationships.

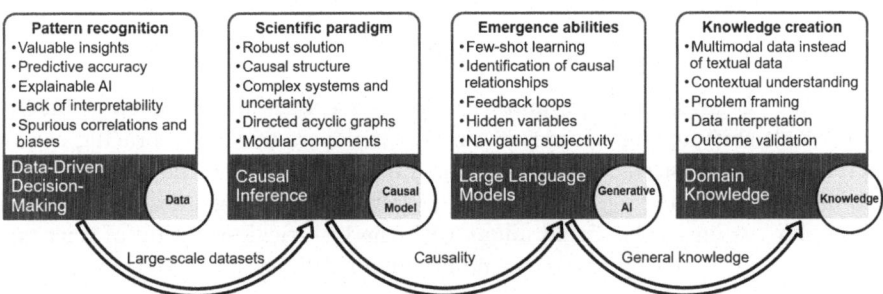

Fig. 1. Heuristic thinking and perspectives from data-driven to causal model-driven decision-making.

As illustrated in Fig. 1, we analyze the inherent limitations of data-driven decision-making and explore the growing interest in alternative paradigms. Notably, it centers on the escalating interest in methodologies anchored in causal inference, with a specific focus on the potential synergies arising from the integration of generative AI and LLMs as a strategic intervention to mitigate the identified limitations.

2.1 Data-Driven Decision-Making and Its Limitations

Organizations leverage statistical learning and machine learning [11] models on large-scale datasets to extract valuable insights aimed at making decisions. Despite the ubiquity of these approaches, their widespread applications have brought several limitations to the fore, particularly within domains where the impact of decisions is critically significant.

A fundamental challenge within data-driven decision-making lies in the balance between predictive accuracy and interpretability [12]. The predilection for purely statistical methodologies often results in models struggling to provide meaningful and understandable explanations. This interpretability deficit not only obstructs the illustration of decision outcomes but also poses a challenge in establishing the requisite trust for decision-making in high-stakes scenarios. Furthermore, the abundant patterns extracted from data may inadvertently include spurious correlations and biases that lack substantive meaning [13]. This sensitivity raises concerns about the reliability of decisions due to the potential for misguided inferences.

Crucially, while the extraction of patterns from data is a powerful capability, it does not inherently translate into the generation of novel knowledge [14]. Distinguishing between pattern recognition [15] and knowledge creation [16] is pivotal, as the former may not necessarily contribute to a deep understanding of the underlying phenomena. This realization underscores the need for a paradigm shift toward an approach that goes beyond mere correlation and enters the domain of causation.

2.2   Causal Inference and Its Benefits

Addressing the acknowledged limitations in data-driven methodologies, there is a noticeable shift among researchers and practitioners toward embracing causal inference as a robust solution [17]. This shift is propelled by the inherent richness of large datasets [18], which reveal patterns simplifying the representation of complex systems. This trend aligns with the historical evolution of scientific thought encapsulated by the scientific paradigm [19], asserting that every phenomenon in the world is causally linked, where actions yield consequences.

Causal inference [20] is the systematic process of elucidating cause-and-effect relationships between variables, aimed at understanding the impact of one variable on another within a given system or context. Constructing models grounded in domain expertise, presented in the form of graphical models such as DAGs [21, 22], enables systematic reasoning about interventions and their effects, thereby enhancing the comprehension of system dynamics and predictive capabilities for formulating new policies.

A fundamental strength of causal inference lies in its capacity to discover relationships between variables, facilitating a deeper understanding of complex system dynamics and revealing novel insights. Furthermore, recent advancements in decision-making have incorporated considerations of uncertainty in both decision theory and optimization methods [23]. The representation of uncertainty significantly influences the expressiveness and tractability of decision models. Analyzing based on causal models proves invaluable in mitigating the impact of uncertainty on decision outcomes and processes. The modular nature of causal models further allows for the systematic development of reusable components, thereby promoting flexibility and adaptability in decision models.

2.3   Large Language Models and Generative AI

Constructing a meaningful and accurate causal model involves overcoming various challenges, including the identification of genuine causal relationships, handling feedback loops and time delays, considering hidden variables, and navigating subjectivity in model building. Despite these challenges, recent advancements with the widespread adoption of LLMs [24] have showcased notable progress, based on pre-training Transformer models [25] on extensive datasets.

Notably, models such as ChatGPT [26] have demonstrated robust capabilities across a spectrum of natural language processing (NLP) tasks, highlighting the potential of LLMs in enhancing decision-making processes. However, a noticeable gap persists in the literature concerning the integration of generative AI and LLMs within the realm of causal inference.

General-purpose LLMs are emerging as foundational tools for generative AI [27], similar to the importance of cloud-native services during the cloud computing era [28]. One notable feature is the *emergence* of exceptional abilities in LLMs [29], contributing to their outstanding performance in generative tasks. Models with few-shot or zero-shot learning capacities, such as GPT-4 [30], present a unique opportunity for efficiently encoding domain expertise into causal models.

2.4   Domain Knowledge in Decision-Making

Domain knowledge holds a central role in decision-making, providing contextual understanding that complements analytical methodologies [31]. This encompasses specialized expertise, insightful perspectives, and specific information relevant to the industry, field, or system under consideration. This wealth of knowledge serves as a cornerstone in problem framing, data interpretation, and outcome validation [32].

The integration of domain knowledge ensures decision-makers grasp the intricacies of a given problem, enabling consideration of subtle aspects that might elude purely data-driven analyses. Past research has predominantly employed either automated or human-in-the-loop approaches for data labeling with human knowledge [33]. However, the process of data annotation may present challenges, requiring domain expertise or involving sensitive data that cannot be crowdsourced, thereby amplifying the difficulty and expense associated with labeling [34].

Methods to inject domain knowledge into data-driven approaches have been explored, utilizing tools such as knowledge graphs, semantic networks, ontology, and NLP [35]. However, these approaches have primarily focused on extracting correlational insights from textual data. In contrast, multimodal LLMs can extract knowledge into causal graphs from various channels, including images, videos, and audio.

3   Methodology

The methodology section outlines our approach to constructing a robust causal model-driven decision-making framework by integrating generative AI capabilities with advanced causal inference techniques. Generative AI extracts structured domain knowledge from diverse datasets and generates candidate causal models, which are iteratively refined through causal discovery algorithms. This comprehensive strategy ensures the infusion of valuable domain knowledge and the creation of modular causal components, thereby enhancing the accuracy, feasibility, and adaptability of the decision-making process.

3.1   Collaborative Development Process

The initiation of our methodological framework involves a collaborative effort between subject experts and state-of-the-art LLMs to contribute domain-specific insights. This expertise is derived from a well-selected textual corpus, denoted as $\mathbb{D} \subseteq \mathbb{U} = \{gd_i\} \cup \{sd_j\}$, where $\mathbb{U}$ represents the universal data, comprising primarily general data gd_i sourced from the Internet (ranging up to TB or PB in volume) and specific data sd_j obtained from domain experts (typically in the order of MB or GB). This corpus encapsulates essential entities $\mathcal{V}$, intricate relationships $\mathcal{R}$, and a set of dynamic attributes $\mathcal{A}$ within the targeted domain. Leveraging the capabilities of advanced LLMs extends beyond surface-level information retrieval, strategically extracting structured knowledge from the datasets and generating an initial set of model components $\mathcal{C}$ (undirected graph G_k representing entities $V_k \subseteq \mathcal{V}$ and relationships $R_k \subseteq \mathcal{R}$) that serve as the foundation for subsequent stages:

$$LLM : \mathbb{D} \to \mathcal{C} = \{< G_k, A > | G_k =< V_k, R_k >, V_k \subseteq \mathcal{V}, R_k \subseteq \mathcal{R}\}$$

where

$$\mathcal{R} \subseteq \{\{x, y\} | < x, y >\in \mathcal{V} \times \mathcal{V}\}$$

$$A = A_V \cup A_R = \bigcup_k \phi_V(V_k) \cup \bigcup_k \phi_E(R_k) \subseteq \mathcal{A}$$

and the attribute functions $\phi_V : V \to \mathcal{P}(A_V)$ assigns to each node $v \in V$ a subset of attributes $\phi_V(v) \subseteq A_V$ and $\phi_E : R \to \mathcal{P}(A_R)$ assigns to each edge $e \in R$ a subset of attributes $\phi_E(e) \subseteq A_R$.

Causal discovery algorithms translate statistical data into a directed causal graph:

$$Causality : \mathcal{C} = \{< G_k, A >\} \to G^0$$

This graph G^0 serves as a foundational structure, visually representing the complex network of relationships within the domain. The results obtained from these models undergo continuous refinement ($G^0 \to G^1 \to \cdots \to G^n$), guided by user feedback and domain experts. This iterative refinement ensures that the derived causal models align with refined domain-specific understanding.

The collaborative approach (Fig. 2) constitutes the bedrock of our methodological framework, intertwining advanced multimodal LLMs, causal discovery algorithms, and human domain-specific expertise. This framework not only extracts knowledge from data but also validates and enhances the knowledge through the advantages of domain-specific expertise, resulting in causal models that are robust, scientifically grounded, and practically applicable.

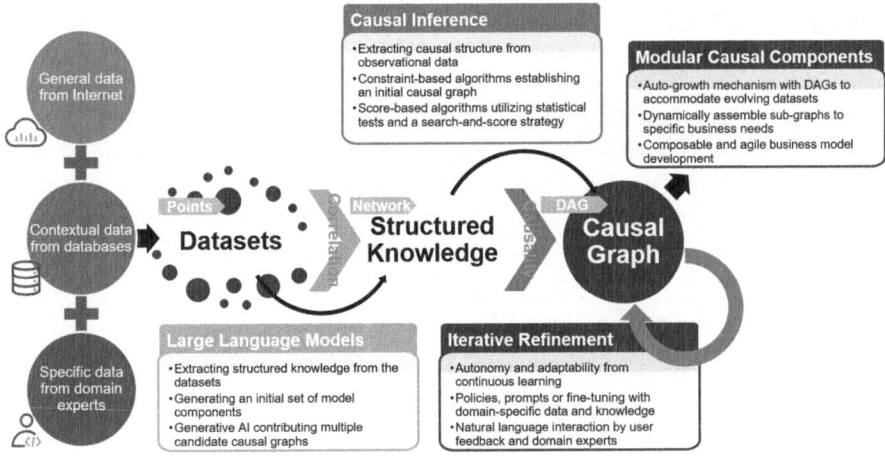

Fig. 2. The methodological framework leverages advanced multimodal LLMs, causal discovery algorithms, and human domain-specific expertise to extract knowledge (Network) and generate a modular causal graph (DAG) from data (Points).

3.2 Synergy Between LLMs and Causal Inference Techniques

The collaborative integration of LLMs and causal inference techniques is a complex and crucial process in the construction of robust decision-making models. At the heart of this integration lies the causal structure G, denoting the collection of causal relationships R among a set of variables V.

Causal discovery is a creative process of extracting causal structure from observational data. Essential causal discovery algorithms include constraint-based algorithms such as the Fast Causal Inference Algorithm (FCI) and score-based algorithms such as the Fast Greedy Equivalence Search (FGES) [36]. These algorithms take center stage in orienting relationships within the model and deriving precise quantitative weights from the available data.

The process begins with constraint-based algorithms establishing an initial causal graph based on conditional independence constraints.

$$FCI : \mathcal{C} = \{< G_k, A >\} \rightarrow G^0 = < V, R, A, L, \phi >$$

where G^0 is a DAG and $\phi : R \rightarrow L$ is a function assigning learning labels such as correlation coefficients to the candidate relationships. For an edge $< x, y > \in R$ and the nodes $x, y \in V$, the start node x is not a child of the end node y in the graph structure G^0.

LLMs and score-based algorithms then collaboratively refine this structure, utilizing statistical tests and a search-and-score strategy, leading to the development and auto-growth of DAGs.

$$FGES : G^0 \xrightarrow{LLM} G^1 \rightarrow \cdots \rightarrow G^n$$

Generative AI contributes by generating multiple candidate causal graphs G_j^i (j is the candidate index in the i-th iteration), and score-based algorithms S assign scores $s_j^i = S(G_j^i)$ to each candidate, ultimately selecting a final graph after n-stages based on these scores $(Optimize(\{G_j^i\}, S) \rightarrow G^i, i = 1, 2, \ldots, n)$.

This collaborative effort ensures an optimizable construction of causal relationships within the model. Each algorithm plays a specific role in enhancing the accuracy and completeness of the causal structure, contributing collectively to the robustness of the overall decision-making model.

3.3   Holistic Incorporation of Domain Knowledge

Domain experts contribute a rich dataset with multimodal inputs, illuminating key concepts and complex mechanisms within the targeted domain. To extract a structured ontology of entities and their relationships, we employ a parsing process utilizing a combination of NLP techniques [37] and computer vision methodologies [38].

Subsequently, textual generation models, driven by this refined ontology, come into play to produce causal model components. These components are dynamic entities capturing the evolving nature of the domain rather than static representations.

While generative AI demonstrates remarkable capabilities, a recognized limitation is its inability to generate entirely new and reliable data beyond the scope of existing knowledge. To address this, the policies [39], prompts [40], or retrieval-augmented generations (RAGs) [41] are introduced to serve as a strategic approach. Moreover, the data governance organizations have the option to fine-tune existing LLMs [42] with domain-specific data and knowledge. This fine-tuning ensures more accurate and contextually appropriate responses, aligning with the intricacies of the domain and allowing for custom transformations provided by domain experts.

The integration of LLMs and causal inference techniques acts as a controller in this process, automating the strategy for applying data and knowledge transformations. This automated control ensures efficiency and consistency in suggesting strategies, thereby enhancing the realism and relevance of the generated data. However, it's crucial to acknowledge potential biases introduced during fine-tuning and to consider the impact of limited data sources on the effectiveness of policies. This provides a more comprehensive understanding of the challenges and considerations in leveraging generative AI within our methodology.

3.4   Enhancing Feasibility Through Modular Causal Components

The model-driven approach presents comprehensive causal models with modular and reusable components structured as DAGs. These dynamic building blocks empower flexible assembly, facilitating swift decision simulation and agile business model development. The introduced modularity is foundational for rapid decision simulation, enabling agile business model development through combinations of pre-defined causal modules. This approach allows practitioners to dynamically assemble sub-graphs, efficiently tailoring decision-making to specific business needs.

Rooted in scientific principles, our methodology instills confidence in its application by fostering efficient experimentation and optimization within decision-making processes. The methodology excels in adapting to diverse domains, utilizing an auto-growth mechanism to accommodate evolving datasets. This ensures robust and relevant decision-making across varying scenarios, seamlessly aligning the model with the ever-changing dynamics of real-world data. This commitment to principled practices significantly contributes to the development of reliable decision-making paradigms.

Consider a scenario such as online sales and customer engagement where modular components are dynamically combined to simulate the impact of various business strategies. This adaptability allows decision-makers to explore diverse scenarios in a controlled environment, optimizing resource allocation and enhancing overall process efficiency. The synergy of modularity, adaptability, and scientific rigor establishes a robust foundation for reliable decision-making models in various domains.

4   Causal Model-Driven Decision-Making Framework

In the domain of decision-making, our framework orchestrates essential processes and components such as data collection, data cleaning, model generation, model validation, and decision support with insightful feedback mechanisms. This process harmonizes three key steps: knowledge ingestion, model simulation, and decision optimization as shown in Fig. 3.

The initial phase involves acquiring data and knowledge from diverse repositories and integrating the capabilities of classical software tools. This raw data then undergoes construction and iterative analysis using causal graphs, while advanced causal inference techniques ensure a rigorous exploration of embedded causal connections.

Insights derived from this phase play a pivotal role in shaping strategies and action plans. The feedback loop seamlessly integrates into business systems, facilitating the assimilation of model-driven decisions into operational processes. This iterative process underscores the framework's efficacy in translating analytical insights into actionable strategies, forming a robust foundation for decision optimization.

4.1   Knowledge Ingestion

The knowledge ingestion phase adopts a classical data-driven approach, collecting raw data from diverse sources, including databases (such as traditional relational databases, NoSQL databases, graph databases, and vector databases), files (semistructured and unstructured data such as text, tables, images, audios, and videos), application programming interfaces (APIs), or web services. Simultaneously, we prioritize data security, implementing encryption measures during the data collection to safeguard sensitive information.

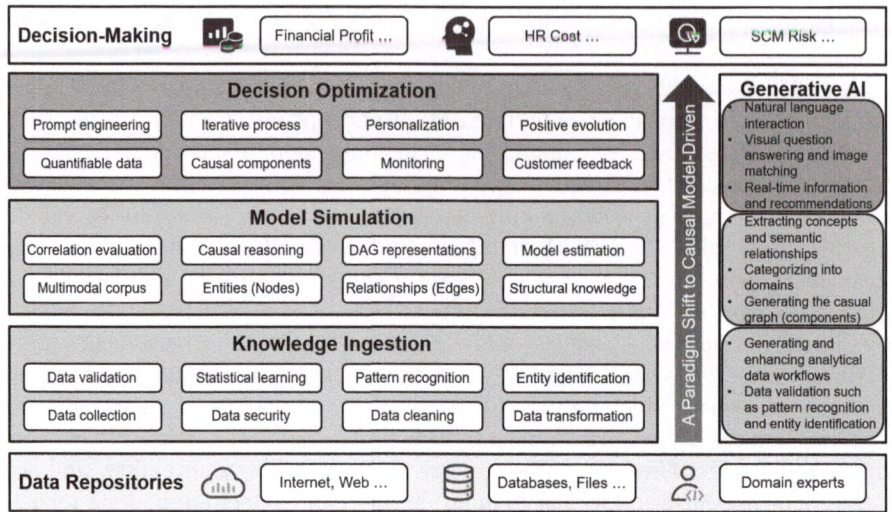

Fig. 3. Causal model-driven decision-making framework with generative AI orchestrates essential processes and components, harmonizing data workflows and feedback mechanisms across knowledge ingestion, model simulation, and decision optimization.

Subsequent processing involves cleaning, transformation, and validation to establish a reliable foundation for decision-making, addressing issues such as duplicate values, missing data, outliers, and proper formatting.

Data validation utilizes traditional statistical methods and machine learning algorithms, revealing patterns and trends for evaluation, error detection, and bias elimination. Aligned with the principles of data-driven architecture, this stage emphasizes data-centric design, real-time processing, and the automation of AI and machine learning.

A significant enhancement is the causal model-driven architecture. The key is the structured knowledge extraction from large-scale multimodal datasets using LLMs and causal discovery algorithms. This results in an initial set of causal model components, which are the foundation for model simulation and decision optimization.

4.2   Model Simulation

This stage involves constructing the causal model using relevant causal discovery algorithms to eliminate biases in causal reasoning, executing model estimation, and conducting verification.

The causal model integrates structural knowledge from datasets, DAG representations from the discovery algorithm, and refined relationships contributed by domain experts. The causal graph is indicative of causality, represented as a DAG graph with nodes and directed edges. Using graph databases and graph analytics frameworks, the causal graph derived from a multimodal corpus becomes easily storable, retrievable, and visualizable.

In typical business scenarios, LLMs extract concepts and their semantic relationships from datasets categorized into domains. Leveraging the capabilities of generative AI, nodes are generated to represent concepts and entities. Augmented by domain knowledge, relationships between these concepts form edges. Nodes and edges populate a graph data structure or database, enabling intuitive analysis or verification.

To accommodate multiple relationships between the same concept pair, multiple edges are generated and assigned similarity weights through correlation evaluation. Causal reasoning consolidates these edges into unique relationships based on causal inference, determining direction and intervention coefficients for one-way connections in the real semantic network. Diverging from traditional knowledge graphs, typically expressed in single-text form, this causal graph integrates information from multimodal data, enriching downstream tasks such as visual question answering and image matching.

Through prototype business use and model validation, clarification objectives and key performance indicators (KPIs) in model-driven decisions undergo assessment. Small-scale cross-validation may also involve alternative machine-learning algorithms. The causal model is subsequently applied to real situations, optimized based on feedback, and evaluated for effective strategy implementation.

4.3   Decision Optimization

In contrast to experiential decision-making, causal model-driven frameworks introduce quantifiable data and optimizable causal model components, establishing a robust foundation for model estimation and optimization. The efficacy of these models, both in components and overall structure, is quantitatively measured by leveraging human domain expertise to assess positive evolution, highlighting synergies between enhanced LLMs and generative AI.

Fueled by data analysis and data visualization, intelligent decision support systems empower business analysts with real-time, precise information and recommendations. For instance, analyzing customers' online behavior and social media activity through causal models and generative AI provides insights to personalize recommendations, tailor marketing strategies, and enhance overall customer satisfaction.

During execution, the system actively monitors fluctuations in business metrics and collects customer feedback. Users engage with LLMs for natural language interaction and prompt engineering, facilitating real-time adjustments and gathering valuable engineering feedback for ongoing decision optimization. This iterative process establishes a continuous optimization loop, extracting insights from action outcomes into data collection and model generation. By fostering the development of flexible and adaptive causal graphs, this approach effectively addresses the limitations of relying solely on data-driven decisions.

5   Applications and Case Studies

The proposed framework underscores its versatility and efficacy in enhancing decision processes across diverse scenarios. It integrates various data sources, generative AI, and causal modeling to extract actionable insights, ensuring relevance across domains and making it a valuable asset for organizations that require scientifically grounded decision-making in dynamic and uncertain environments.

5.1   Financial Profit Analysis

We begin with comprehensive data ingestion, including transactions, market trends, and economic indicators. Causal inference techniques are then employed to reveal latent patterns within the complex financial landscape.

Next, we construct a financial causal model by integrating structural domain knowledge and leveraging generative AI capabilities for simulation under various scenarios. This iterative simulation process refines the model, enabling financial analysts to understand the impact of decisions on profit outcomes.

Insights derived from the model simulations are translated into actionable strategies, considering factors such as risk tolerance and current market conditions. This strategic synergy between LLMs and causal inference produces optimized decision pathways, allowing for adaptive adjustments to investment portfolios and market strategies.

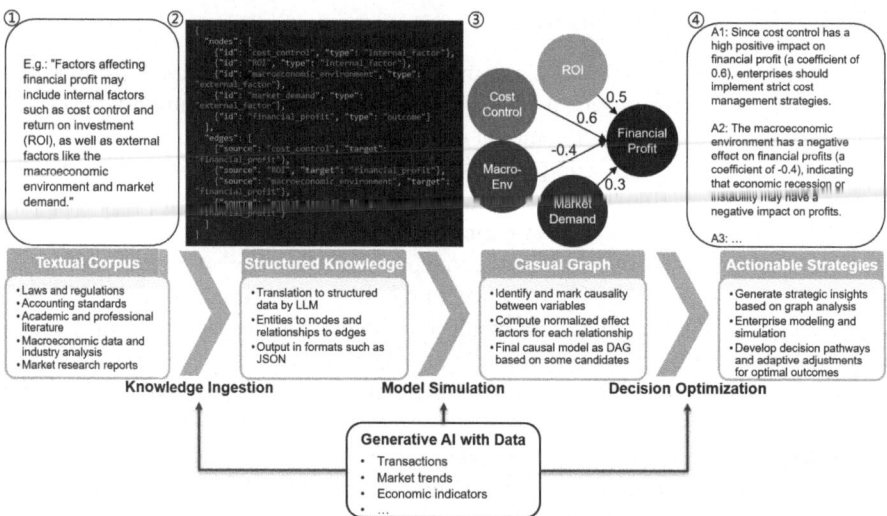

Fig. 4. The workflow and business process of decision-making in financial profit analysis driven by the causal model with a simple example.

As shown in Fig. 4, these enhancements lead to augmented predictive capabilities, proactive decision-making, and strengthened risk management strategies.

These improvements significantly contribute to increased financial performance and organizational agility in navigating market fluctuations.

5.2   HR Cost Analysis

Human resources (HR) datasets encompass employee demographics, performance metrics, and compensation structures. The knowledge ingestion process analyzes complex connections within the HR domain, uncovering relationships that significantly impact HR costs.

In the model simulation phase, the framework constructs an HR causal model by integrating domain expertise and leveraging generative AI capabilities. This iterative process refines the model, equipping HR analysts with predictive capabilities to optimize HR expenditures.

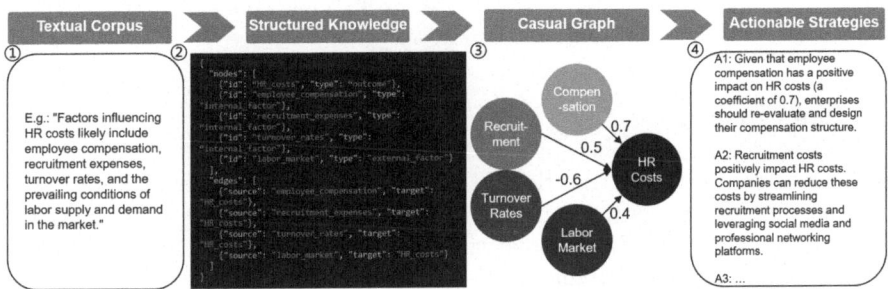

Fig. 5. The workflow and business process of decision-making in HR cost analysis.

In the decision optimization phase, simulation outcomes are translated into strategic initiatives for HR cost control, tailoring strategies to evolving organizational goals and external market dynamics. As illustrated in Fig. 5, the framework's adaptability enhances responsiveness to changing workforce trends, contributing substantively to informed decision-making and proactive cost-control measures.

5.3   SCM Risk Analysis

To identify risks and uncertainties, a diverse range of repositories within supply chain management (SCM) is required. Causal inference techniques uncover potential dependencies, providing a holistic view of the interconnected elements influencing supply chain risks.

The causal model encapsulates the dynamic interactions of supply chain elements, simulating various risk scenarios and empowering stakeholders to anticipate and strategize responses. By leveraging causal inference, the framework identifies optimal risk mitigation measures, incorporating real-time data and feedback to enable proactive decision-making.

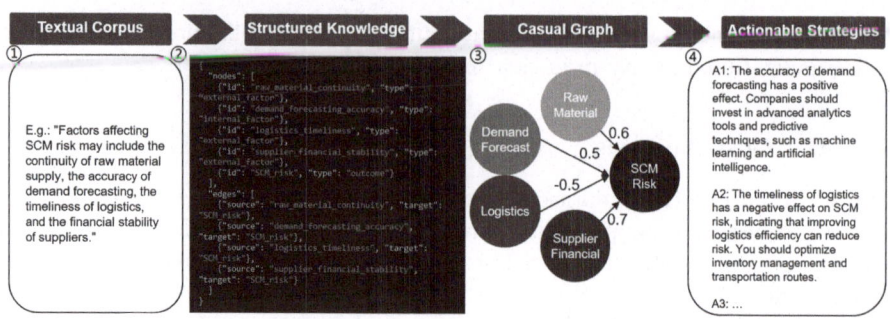

Fig. 6. The workflow and business process of decision-making in SCM risk analysis.

As illustrated in Fig. 6, targeted strategies effectively mitigate risks, ensuring continuous improvement and contributing to a resilient and responsive supply chain capable of withstanding challenges.

6   Conclusions

Demand is shifting from traditional reactive reporting to actionable, proactive insights, emphasizing optimization, advanced techniques, and composable business analytics. The growing popularity of graph techniques provides an excellent foundation for decision intelligence and prescriptive analytics. Causal graphs highlight early signals, causality links, and pathways forward, facilitating the implementation of decisions and actions.

However, the limitations of data-driven approaches in establishing causal relationships pose a significant challenge for decision-makers tackling complex real-world problems. To address this issue, our investigation explores a causal model-driven decision-making framework, revealing its potential to cultivate a composable and intelligent business model. At its core, this framework integrates generative AI, statistical methods, and domain expertise. Represented typically by causal graphs, the model benefits from the extraction, generation, and expansion of a semantic network derived from both structured and unstructured data. The flexibility afforded by composable causal graphs forms the foundation for comprehensive decision-making in complex environments.

In conclusion, the causal model-driven decision-making framework offers a robust and principled paradigm for reliable decision-making by integrating generative AI with causal inference techniques. However, several challenges must be addressed for broader practical adoption, particularly in mitigating biases, ensuring model effectiveness, and managing ethical considerations:

- *Biases:* Input from domain experts and generative AI can introduce biases from personal perspectives, cognitive limitations, or subjective data interpretations. Mitigating these biases is essential to preserve objectivity and fairness in decision models.

- *Effectiveness:* The framework's effectiveness depends on the data quality and representativeness. Inaccurate decisions may result from incomplete or outdated datasets, requiring continuous model refinement. Empirical validation and comparative analysis with existing methods would further solidify the framework's effectiveness.
- *Ethics:* With increasing reliance on data, ethical concerns around privacy, consent, and responsible AI use become critical. Adhering to ethical standards and regulatory frameworks is imperative, demanding transparency and accountability in deployment to address potential societal impacts.

Future research should focus on comprehensive evaluations through large-scale experiments, demonstrating the framework's performance in various real-world scenarios. Incorporating more explicit examples that illustrate the construction of causal models in specific domains will enhance its practical relevance. Exploring synergies between causal models and emerging technologies such as smart contracts and federated learning could further strengthen the decision-making framework and broaden its applications in innovative fields.

Acknowledgments. This work is supported by the Shenzhen Science and Technology Program (Grant No. KJZD20231023094501003), the National Key R&D Program of China (Grant No. 2023YFB3308502), the Shenzhen Sustainable Development Science and Technology Project (Grant No. KCXST20221021111201002), and the Key-Area R&D Program of Guangdong Province, China (Grant No. 2020B0101090003).

References

1. McAfee, A., et al.: Big data: the management revolution. Harv. Bus. Rev. **90**(10), 60–68 (2012)
2. Yaqoob, I., et al.: Big data: from beginning to future. Int. J. Inf. Manage. **36**(6), 1231–1247 (2016). https://doi.org/10.1016/j.ijinfomgt.2016.07.009
3. Jeble, S., Kumari, S., Patil, Y.: Role of big data in decision making. Oper. Supply Chain Manage. Int. J. **11**(1), 36–44 (2017). https://doi.org/10.31387/oscm0300198
4. Brynjolfsson, E., McElheran, K.: The rapid adoption of data-driven decision-making. Am. Econ. Rev. **106**(5), 133–139 (2016). https://doi.org/10.1257/aer.p20161016
5. Xu, F., Uszkoreit, H., Du, Y., Fan, W., Zhao, D., Zhu, J.: Explainable AI: a brief survey on history, research areas, approaches and challenges. In: Tang, J., Kan, M.-Y., Zhao, D., Li, S., Zan, H. (eds.) NLPCC 2019. LNCS (LNAI), vol. 11839, pp. 563–574. Springer, Cham (2019). https://doi.org/10.1007/978-3-030-32236-6_51
6. Dane, E., Pratt, M.G.: Exploring intuition and its role in managerial decision making. Acad. Manag. Rev. **32**(1), 33–54 (2007). https://doi.org/10.5465/amr.2007.23463682
7. Pearl, J.: Causal diagrams for empirical research. Biometrika **82**(4), 669–688 (1995). https://doi.org/10.1093/biomet/82.4.669
8. Pearl, J.: Causal inference in statistics: an overview. Statist. Surv. **3**, 96–146 (2009). https://doi.org/10.1214/09-SS057
9. Pearl, J.: The foundations of causal inference. Sociol. Methodol. **40**(1), 75–149 (2010). https://doi.org/10.1111/j.1467-9531.2010.01228.x

10. Scheer, A.W.: The composable enterprise: agile, flexible, innovative: a gamechanger for organisations. Digitisation and Business Software. Springer Nature (2023). https://doi.org/10.1007/978-3-658-43089-4

11. Jordan, M.I., Mitchell, T.M.: Machine learning: trends, perspectives, and prospects. Science **349**(6245), 255–260 (2015). https://doi.org/10.1126/science.aaa8415

12. He, C., Ma, M., Wang, P.: Extract interpretability-accuracy balanced rules from artificial neural networks: A review. Neurocomputing **387**, 346–358 (2020). https://doi.org/10.1016/j.neucom.2020.01.036

13. Geirhos, R., et al.: Shortcut learning in deep neural networks. Nature Mach. Intell. **2**(11), 665–673 (2020). https://doi.org/10.1038/s42256-020-00257-z

14. Cao, Y., et al.: A comprehensive survey of ai-generated content (aigc): A history of generative ai from gan to chatgpt. arXiv preprint arXiv:2303.04226 (2023). https://doi.org/10.48550/arXiv.2303.04226

15. Jain, A.K., Duin, R.P.W., Mao, J.: Statistical pattern recognition: a review. IEEE Trans. Pattern Anal. Mach. Intell. **22**(1), 4–37 (2000). https://doi.org/10.1109/34.824819

16. Lambiotte, R., Panzarasa, P.: Communities, knowledge creation, and information diffusion. J. Informet. **3**(3), 180–190 (2009). https://doi.org/10.1016/j.joi.2009.03.007

17. Bareinboim, E., Pearl, J.: Causal inference and the data-fusion problem. Proc. Natl. Acad. Sci. **113**(27), 7345–7352 (2016). https://doi.org/10.1073/pnas.1510507113

18. Thai, H.T.: Machine learning for structural engineering: a state-of-the-art review. Structures **38**, 448–491 (2022). https://doi.org/10.1016/j.istruc.2022.02.003

19. Ginzburg, C.: Clues: roots of a scientific paradigm. Theory Soc. **7**(3), 273–288 (1979). https://www.jstor.org/stable/656747

20. Pearl, J.: Causality. Cambridge University Press (2009)

21. Textor, J., et al.: Robust causal inference using directed acyclic graphs: the R package 'dagitty'. Int. J. Epidemiol. **45**(6), 1887–1894 (2016). https://doi.org/10.1093/ije/dyw341

22. Peters, J., Bühlmann, P.: Structural intervention distance for evaluating causal graphs. Neural Comput. **27**(3), 771–799 (2015). https://doi.org/10.1162/NECO_a_00708

23. Keith, A.J., Ahner, D.K.: A survey of decision making and optimization under uncertainty. Ann. Oper. Res. **300**(2), 319–353 (2019). https://doi.org/10.1007/s10479-019-03431-8

24. Zhao, W.X., et al.: A survey of large language models. arXiv preprint arXiv:2303.18223 (2023). https://doi.org/10.48550/arXiv.2303.18223

25. Vaswani, A., et al.: Attention is all you need. Advances in Neural Information Processing Systems **30** (2017)

26. Ray, P.P.: ChatGPT: a comprehensive review on background, applications, key challenges, bias, ethics, limitations and future scope. Internet Things Cyber-Phys. Syst. **3**, 121–154 (2023). https://doi.org/10.1016/j.iotcps.2023.04.003

27. Epstein, Z., et al.: Art and the science of generative AI. Science **380**(6650), 1110–1111 (2023). https://doi.org/10.1038/d41586-023-00340-6

28. Zhang, L.J., Zhou, Q.: CCOA: cloud computing open architecture. In: Proceedings of 2009 IEEE International Conference on Web Services (ICWS), pp. 607–616. IEEE (2009). https://doi.org/10.1109/ICWS.2009.144

29. Wei, J., et al.: Emergent abilities of large language models. arXiv preprint arXiv:2206.07682 (2022). https://doi.org/10.48550/arXiv.2206.07682

30. Achiam, J., et al.: GPT-4 Technical Report. arXiv preprint arXiv:2303.08774 (2023). https://doi.org/10.48550/arXiv.2303.08774

31. Courtney, J.F.: Decision making and knowledge management in inquiring organizations: toward a new decision-making paradigm for DSS. Decis. Support Syst. **31**(1), 17–38 (2001). https://doi.org/10.1016/S0167-9236(00)00117-2

32. Baer, J.: The importance of domain-specific expertise in creativity. Roeper Rev. **37**(3), 165–178 (2015). https://doi.org/10.1080/02783193.2015.1047480

33. Wu, X., et al.: A survey of human-in-the-loop for machine learning. Futur. Gener. Comput. Syst. **135**, 364–381 (2022). https://doi.org/10.1016/j.future.2022.05.014

34. Liang, W., et al.: Advances, challenges and opportunities in creating data for trustworthy AI. Nature Mach. Intell. **4**(8), 669–677 (2022). https://doi.org/10.1038/s42256-022-00516-1

35. Chen, H., Luo, X.: An automatic literature knowledge graph and reasoning network modeling framework based on ontology and natural language processing. Adv. Eng. Inform. **42**, 100959 (2019). https://doi.org/10.1016/j.aei.2019.100959

36. Shen, X., et al.: Challenges and opportunities with causal discovery algorithms: application to Alzheimer's pathophysiology. Sci. Rep. **10**(1), 2975 (2020). https://doi.org/10.1038/s41598-020-59669-x

37. Ning, Y., et al.: A review of deep learning based speech synthesis. Appl. Sci. **9**(19), 4050 (2019). https://doi.org/10.3390/app9194050

38. Jiang, F., Chen, H., Zhang, L.J.: FCN-biLSTM based VAT invoice recognition and processing. In: Liu, S., Tekinerdogan, B., Aoyama, M., Zhang, LJ. (eds.) EDGE 2018. LNCS, vol. 10973, pp. 135–143. Springer, Cham. (2018). https://doi.org/10.1007/978-3-319-94340-4_11

39. Ratner, A.J., et al.: Learning to compose domain-specific transformations for data augmentation. Advances in Neural Information Processing Systems **30** (2017)

40. Reynolds, L., McDonell, K.: Prompt programming for large language models: beyond the few-shot paradigm. In: Extended Abstracts of the 2021 CHI Conference on Human Factors in Computing Systems, pp. 1–7, May 2021. https://doi.org/10.1145/3411763.3451760

41. Lewis, P., et al.: Retrieval-augmented generation for knowledge-intensive nlp tasks. Adv. Neural. Inf. Process. Syst. **33**, 9459–9474 (2020)

42. Bakker, M., et al.: Fine-tuning language models to find agreement among humans with diverse preferences. Adv. Neural. Inf. Process. Syst. **35**, 38176–38189 (2022)

Incorporating Feature Refinement Enhancement and Cross Network for Click-Through Rate Prediction

Sumin Li$^{(\boxtimes)}$ ⓘ, Zhen Xie ⓘ, Na Sun ⓘ, and Hengming Cao ⓘ

School of Information Engineering, Minzu University of China, Beijing, China
smli@muc.edu.cn

Abstract. Click-through rate(CTR) prediction is an important task in personalized advertising and recommender systems. Currently, many approaches model feature interactions to improve their performance. DeepFM as a classical approach takes care of both high-order and low-order feature interactions in a parallel way, but it has some limitations. Firstly, it ignores the fact that the importance of the same feature may be different in different contexts, and secondly, it has a limited number of orders of explicit feature interactions and the importance of feature interactions is not differentiated. To address these issues, we improve DeepFM and propose FRGCN, a click rate prediction model that combines feature refinement enhancement with cross network; specifically, we add an attention-based feature refinement enhancement layer FRNet-A after the embedding layer to achieve context-aware representation of features and attention enhancement. In addition, we introduce gated cross network instead of FM modules in the feature interaction layer to capture higher-order explicit feature interactions. Comprehensive experimental results on Frappe and Malware datasets demonstrate the effectiveness and superiority of FRGCN.

Keywords: Click-through Rate Prediction · Feature Interaction · Feature Refinement Enhancement · Cross Network

1 Introduction

Click-through rate (CTR) prediction has become an important task in real-world applications such as recommender systems and online advertising [1]. It aims to predict the probability of users clicking on specific content. Accurate CTR prediction can help content providers optimize their resource allocation and increase revenues, while enhancing user experience and improving user satisfaction [2]. Typically, a click-through rate prediction model consists of embedding layer, feature interaction layer, and prediction layer [3]. Many approaches have achieved great success by targeting the feature interaction layer and using different ways of modeling feature interactions as an entry point [4–6]. Many traditional methods such as logistic regression (LR) [7] and FM-based methods [8–11] can only

© The Author(s), under exclusive license to Springer Nature Switzerland AG 2025
X. Pan et al. (Eds.): AIMS 2024, LNCS 15421, pp. 20–34, 2025.
https://doi.org/10.1007/978-3-031-77681-6_2

model low-order feature interactions. As deep learning techniques have been applied and made great progress in many research areas, the use of Deep Neural Networks (DNN) to implicitly model higher-order feature interactions is also a research trend in the CTR field [2,12,13]. Some recent approaches [5,6,14] using cross networks for explicit feature interaction while taking into account implicit higher-order feature interaction have achieved good results.

Deep Factorization Machine (DeepFM) [12], is an architecture that integrates a factorization machine and a deep neural network in a parallel manner, and is able to take into account both higher-order and lower-order feature interactions. The FM part models the low-order feature interactions and the DNN part models the high-order feature interactions. Although the above method can effectively improve the accuracy of click rate prediction, it ignores the fact that the importance of the same feature is different in different contexts. For example, the feature "male" has different importance in *male, basketball* and *male, lipstick*, and this difference should be taken into account in the feature representation. In addition to this, the FM part models explicit feature interactions of limited order and the importance of all feature interactions is not differentiated.

To address the above problems, we propose a click-through rate prediction model FRGCN that incorporates feature refinement enhancement and cross network to improve DeepFM. Specifically, we first add an attention mechanism-based feature refinement enhancement layer FRNet-A after the embedding layer to realize the context-aware representation of features and perform attention enhancement. The FRNet-A layer is based on FRNet [15] and combines the multi-head self-attention mechanism to realize the attention-enhanced feature representation; moreover, we introduce the gated cross network GCN [6] in the feature interaction layer instead of the FM module, which can capture explicit interactions within bounded degree and at the same time selectively amplify important feature interactions, effectively compensating for the shortcomings of the FM module. Comprehensive experiments show that FRGCN has good performance on both datasets and effectively improves the click rate prediction.

The rest of the paper is organized as follows: related work is presented in Sect. 2. Section 3 describes the proposed FRGCN model in detail. Experimental results are shown and discussed in Sect. 4. Section 5 summarizes the paper.

2   Related Work

Initially CTR prediction was mainly done using traditional binary classification methods commonly used in machine learning, such as LR [7], learning the corresponding weight coefficients for each feature, but this model cannot do adaptive feature interaction, can only focus on the first-order feature information, and has poor expressive ability. Attentional Factorization Machine (AFM) [16], which adaptively learns the importance of feature interactions by introducing attentional weights; Lian et al. designed the xDeepFM [13], which improves on DeepFM, mainly because the Compressed Interaction Network (CIN) explicitly learns higher-order crossover features with a learning granularity of vector dimensions. In addition, some studies have focused on different methods of feature representation to improve CTR prediction. IFM [11], which uses Factor Estimation Network(FEN) to improve FM by learning vector-level weights for different feature representations. FiBiNET [17] uses squeeze and excitation networks to extract informative features by re-weighting the original features. FRNet [15] modeling by nonlinear context-aware feature representation for better performance.

CTR prediction models generally use Multilayer Perceptron (MLP) to implement implicit higher-order feature interactions. Meanwhile, many different approaches to implement explicit higher-order feature interactions have appeared. AutoInt [4] uses a multi-head self-attentive neural network to explicitly model feature combinations in a low-dimensional space. InterHAt [18] captures higher-order feature combinations through an efficient attention aggregation strategy with "low computational complexity". DCN [14] uses cross network to capture explicit feature interactions with bounded degree. The later proposed DCN V2 [5], improves the performance of DCN when modeling complex explicit crossovers. GDCN [6] uses the Gated Cross Network to capture explicit higher-order feature interactions and filter important feature interactions dynamically by adding information gates at each order of crossover layer. Based on the aforementioned research, we creatively combined the cross network with the attention-enhanced feature refinement network to improve existing models, achieving better performance.

3   Proposed Model

In this paper, we propose the FRGCN model, which consists of an embedding layer, a feature refinement enhancement layer(FRNet-A) based on the attention mechanism, a feature interaction layer, and a prediction layer. The embedding layer converts high-dimensional sparse inputs into low-dimensional dense vectors; FRNet-A layer generates context-aware representations of the features and performs attentional enhancement on them; feature interaction layer performs explicit and implicit interactions with the features; and the prediction layer concatenates the outputs of the explicit and implicit parts as the inputs for predicting click-through-rates. The structure of FRGCN is shown in Fig. 1.

3.1   Embedding Layer

The input data for the CTR task usually consists of sparse features, which are typically encoded as one-hot vectors as follows:

$$x = [x_1, x_2, ..., x_m], \tag{1}$$

where m denotes the number of fields, and $x_i \in \mathbb{R}^n$ denotes the one-hot vector of categorized fields with n features and the feature embedding E_i of the one-hot vector x_i is obtained using (2):

$$E_i = W_i x_i, \tag{2}$$

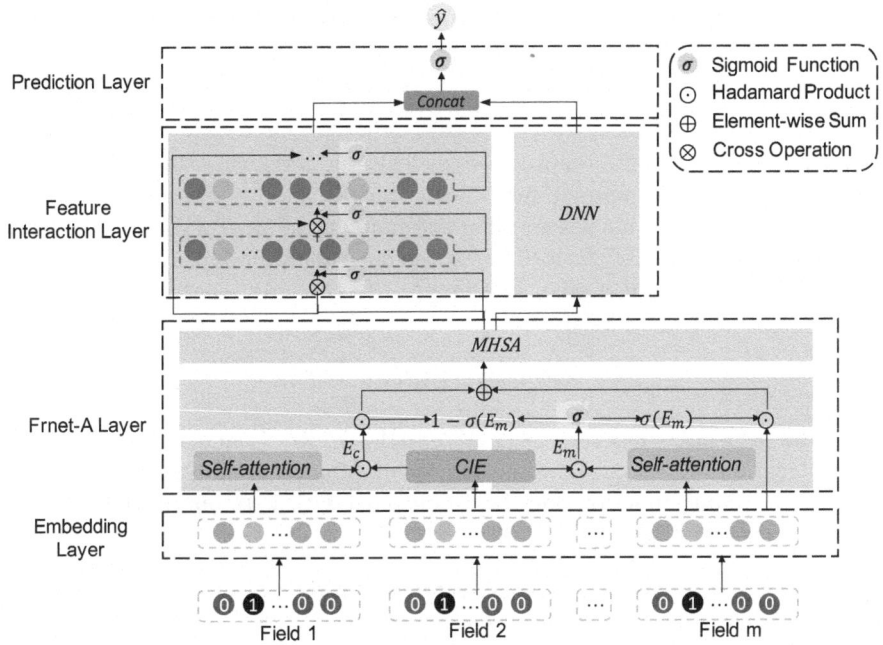

Fig. 1. Structure of FRGCN.

where $W_i \in \mathbb{R}^{d \times n}$ denotes the embedding matrix of x_i and $E_i \in \mathbb{R}^d$ denotes the embedding of a field with an embedding dimension of d.

By the above method, he high latitude and sparse feature input vectors are compressed into low dimensional and dense vectors. And the result of the original features output through the embedding layer can be expressed as:

$$E = concat(E_1, ..., E_i, ..., E_m) \in \mathbb{R}^{m \times d}. \tag{3}$$

3.2   FRNet-A Layer

FRNet-A, proposed in this paper, consists of the following three main components:

- Information Extraction Unit (IEU): This module fully extracts contextual information contained in all features and relationships across features.
- Complementary Selection Gate (CSGate): This module combines the original significant features and complementary features to generate context-aware feature representations.
- Multi-Headed Self-Attention Enhancement Module (MHSA): Enhanced representation of features using multiple attention heads to create different subspaces and learn feature correlations under different subspaces respectively.

Information Extraction Unit. This part includes Self-attention module(Self-attention) and Contextual Information Extractor(CIE). The IEU enables the extraction of contextual information and attention to cross-feature relationships. Specifically:

Self-attention. This module captures cross-feature relationships by evaluating the correlation between all pairs of features in order to identify the feature with the highest correlation to that feature. For example, in the case of *Male, Basketball, Eye Shadow*, the feature "*Basketball*" is the most relevant feature to the feature "*Male*". First, the input matrix E is mapped to three different matrices by (4): Q(query), K(key) and V(Value).

$$Q = EW_Q, K = EW_K, V = EW_V, \tag{4}$$

where the projection matrix $W_Q \in \mathbb{R}^{d \times d_k}$, $W_K \in \mathbb{R}^{d \times d_k}$ and $W_V \in \mathbb{R}^{d \times d_k}$. d_k is the attention factor. Afterwards, the dot product of Q and K is normalized using the *Softmax* function and then multiplied with V to obtain the attention matrix as shown in (5).

$$O_{Att} = Softmax(QK^T)V \in \mathbb{R}^{m \times d_k}. \tag{5}$$

After that, the dimension of the output matrix is transformed to be the same as the input by the projection matrix $W_P \in \mathbb{R}^{d_k \times d}$. Finally, the output O_{att} of the self-attention module is obtained.

$$O_{att} = O_{Att}W_P \in \mathbb{R}^{m \times d}. \tag{6}$$

Contextual Information Extractor. This module ensures that the contextual information implicitly included in all features for a given instance is extracted. Since context information is generally relatively simple, MLP is chosen to extract the context information. Before that we flatten the matrix E to get $E_f \in \mathbb{R}^{1 \times (m*d)}$. The procedure is shown in Fig. 2.

Using E_f as the input to the MLP, the inputs to each layer of the MLP are obtained through (7). Using the *ReLU* function as the activation function,

$$L_{i+1} = Relu(M_i L_i + b_i). \tag{7}$$

Among them L_i and L_{i+1} are the ith and $(i+1)^{th}$ hidden layers and $L_0 = E_f \in \mathbb{R}^{1 \times (m*d)}$ is the first hidden layer. M_i is the weight matrix of the ith hidden layer, and b_i is the learned parameter of the ith hidden layer. In the last hidden layer the dimensions of the context information vector are projected to the d (dimension of embedding size) to get the final context information vector $O_{bit} \in \mathbb{R}^{1 \times d}$.

O_{bit} contains all the information obtained from E_f to represent the context information of a particular instance. Since different instances contain different features, for each instance the context information O_{bit} is unique for each instance.

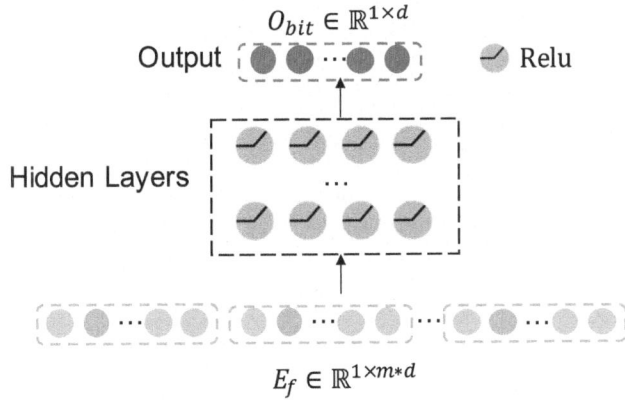

Fig. 2. The structure of CIE.

Finally, we use the contextual information O_{bit} to the output of the self-attention module O_{att} weighted representation so that each feature can have different representations in different situations, as shown in (8):

$$E_m = O_{att} \odot O_{bit} \in \mathbb{R}^{m \times d}. \qquad (8)$$

Complementary Selection Gate. We multiply the IEU to generate complementary features so that we can better enrich the feature space, and this module we refer to as the IEU_C. To better utilize the weight matrix E_m to select important feature information from the original embedded features and supplementary features, a gate mechanism is used to control the information flow. Input the original features E, weight matrix E_m and the supplementary features generated by the IEU_C module into the gate. After (9) combines the original important features and supplementary features, the final feature space-rich feature representation with contextual information $E_{context} \in \mathbb{R}^{m \times d}$, which we take as input to the feature interaction layer.

$$E_{context} = E \odot \sigma(E_m) + E_c \odot (1 - \sigma(E_m)). \qquad (9)$$

where $\sigma(\cdot)$ is the *Sigmoid* function, and each element in $\sigma(E_m)$ denotes the importance of the corresponding element in the matrix E, and $1 - \sigma(E_m)$ denotes another part of the contextual features. The gate mechanism is utilized to achieve adaptive balance between the original and supplementary features.

Multi-headed Self-attention Enhancement Module. We augment $E_{context}$ further using a multi-head self-attention mechanism. By using multiple heads to create different subspaces, the feature relevance of features under different subspaces is learned separately. After using (4) (5) (6), we can get the output of a certain attention head, i.e., $head_i$, which represents the features under the ith

subspace learned by the multi-head self-attention mechanism [19]. We combine different features learned by multiple heads (assumed to be n) under different subspaces as shown in (10):

$$Head = concat(head_1, head_2, ..., head_n). \tag{10}$$

As Fig. 3 Shown, the number of heads is taken as 2. While computing the multi-head attention, in order to preserve the initial information of the input vector, we combine the residual network to preserve the original input information as well. The output is shown in (11), and

$$E_{context\_A} = MHSA(E_{context}) = Relu(Head + W_{Res}E_{context}) \in \mathbb{R}^{m \times d}, \tag{11}$$

where W_{Res} is the projection matrix for the dimension mismatch case.

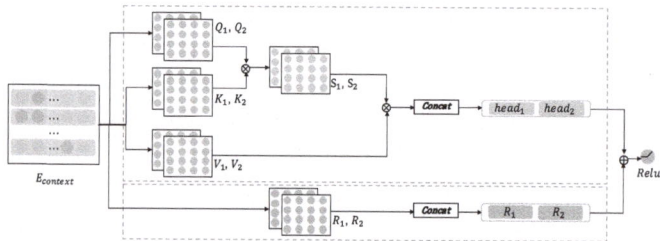

Fig. 3. Schematic diagram of MHSA mechanism. It consists of a multi-head self-attention mechanism component and a residual network component.

3.3   Feature Interaction Layer

In this section we introduce the gated cross network GCN [6] instead of FM to implement explicit higher-order feature interactions, whose formulae for each layer are summarized below:

$$l_i = l_0 \odot (W_{i-1}^l \times l_{i-1} + b_{i-1}) \odot \sigma(W_{i-1}^g \times l_{i-1}) + l_{i-1}. \tag{12}$$

where $l_0 \in \mathbb{R}^{1 \times (m*d)}$ is the spreading input from the FRNet-A layer; l_{i-1} is the output from the previous gated cross layer and is used as the input of the current l_i layer, $l_i \in \mathbb{R}^{1 \times (m*d)}$ is the output of the current layer; $\sigma(\cdot)$ is the *sigmoid* function; b_{i-1} is the bias, and W_{i-1}^l and W_{i-1}^g are two learnable matrices. Where W_{i-1}^l is also known as the cross matrix, which represents the importance between the individual feature domains in the current i^{th} order. Since not all of the $(i+1)^{th}$ order features have a positive impact on prediction, information gates are used to adaptively learn the importance of the $(i+1)^{th}$ order features. This process amplifies the role played by important features. And as the number of cross network layers increases, the information gate at each cross network layer filters the next order crossover features, effectively controlling the flow of information [6]. Meanwhile, we use MLP as DNN to implement implicit higher-order feature interactions, and each hidden layer is represented as shown in (7).

3.4 Prediction Layer

Denote the two parts of the output of the feature interaction layer as O_{cross} and O_{mlp}. Connecting the two parts of the output, the process can be visualized as

$$O = [O_{\text{cross}} \parallel O_{\text{mlp}}]. \tag{13}$$

Finally, we compute the predicted click probability $\hat{y}_i$ by a standard logistic regression function i.e.,

$$\hat{y}_i = \sigma(W_{logit}O) \in (0,1), \tag{14}$$

where $\sigma(\cdot)$ is the *sigmoid* function, and W_{logit} is the weight vector.

The loss function needs to be minimized during the training process, and the loss function in this paper uses the cross-entropy loss function as shown below:

$$Logloss = -\frac{1}{N} \sum_{j=1}^{N} y_i \log(\hat{y}_i) + (1 - y_i) \log(1 - \hat{y}_i), \tag{15}$$

where N denotes the total number of samples for training, the y_i and $\hat{y}_i$ denote the real click rate and predicted click rate, respectively.

4 Experimentation

4.1 Experimental Setup

Dataset Information. We chose two widely used datasets to evaluate our proposed approach against other CTR models, namely Frappe [20–22] and Malware [23]. The Frappe dataset contains data on users' usage behavior on mobile apps, with labeled values indicating whether or not the user has used the app in that context. The Malware dataset is published in the Microsoft Malware Forecast for predicting the probability that a Windows computer will be infected, and can be represented as a binary classification problem with 81 different fields. Each dataset is divided in the ratio (training set: validation set: test set) of 7:2:1. The statistics of these datasets are shown in Table 1.

Table 1. Dataset information statistics.

Datasets	Training	Validation	Testing	Features	Fields
Frappe	202027	57722	28860	5382	10
Malware	6245037	1784297	892149	976208	81

Evaluation Indicators. In this paper, AUC (Area Under ROC Curve) and Logloss (Logistic loss) are used to evaluate the performance of all models in the test set. An increase or decrease in both AUC and Logloss at the 0.001 level is considered to be a significant improvement in the CTR prediction task [13,15,17].

Comparative Model. In order to evaluate our approach, we compare the proposed FRGCN model with other mainstream models and we categorize it into three categories respectively:

1) First Order Methods, LR [7];
2) Methods for modeling second-order cross features based on FM, including FM [8], IFM [24], DIFM [10];
3) Methods for capturing higher-order crossover features, including NFM [22], IPNN [25], DCN [14], FiBiNET [17], DeepFM [12], xDeepFM [13], AutoInt+ [26], AFN+ [21], DCN-V2 [5], GDCN [6], DeepFM$_{FRNet}$ [15].

Experimental Details. We use Pytorch to implement the above model. A cached database is introduced for better reading of the data and the cross-entropy loss function is optimized using Adam optimizer. During training, the default learning rate is 0.01 and 0.001 on Frappe and Malware datasets, respectively, and if the evaluation metrics stop improving in four consecutive periods, the learning rate is reduced to 0.0001 by the Reduce-LR-On-Plateau scheduler. When the logloss on the validation set stops improving, this paper uses an early stopping to avoid overfitting situations. The batchsize is set to 4096 in the experiments. The embedding size of the embedding layer is set to 20 on the Frappe dataset, and is set to 10 on the Malware dataset. Based on previous work [6,15], this paper uses a uniform setting (i.e., 3 layers, 400-400-400) for models involving MLPs for fair comparison.

4.2   Experimental Results and Analysis

Comparison of Model Performance. The overall performance of each model on Frappe and Malware is summarized in Table 2. First, on both datasets, the AUC of FRGCN is 0.50% and 0.59% higher than that of DeepFM, and the Logloss is 14.52% and 0.63% lower than that of DeepFM, which suggests that the addition of the additive feature refinement enhancement layer and the introduction of the cross-network in place of FM is effective. This indicates that the fusion of the two modules is more effective than using them individually. Secondly, we can find that in most cases, the model performance of higher-order feature interactions performs due to the model of lower-order feature interactions, indicating that it is effective to improve the model performance by learning complex higher-order feature interactions. Finally, on the Frappe dataset, the AUC of FRGCN (Logloss of 5.55% and 4.42%) outperforms the values of GDCN and DeepFM$_{FRNet}$ by 0.25% and 0.20%; on the Malware dataset, the AUC of FRGCN (Logloss of 0.49% and 0.19%) outperforms the values of GDCN and DeepFM$_{FRNet}$ of 0.45% and 0.38%.

Hyperparametric Experiments. In this subsection, experimental analyses will be conducted on the Frappe and Malware real datasets for several key hyperparameters in the FRGCN model of this paper, i.e., the number of heads, the

Table 2. Comparison of overall performance of CTR models.

Model	Frappe		Malware	
	AUC	Logloss	AUC	Logloss
LR	0.9376	0.2882	0.7107	0.6196
FM	0.9708	0.1934	0.7309	0.6052
IFM	0.9765	0.1896	0.7389	0.5969
DIFM	0.9788	0.1860	0.7397	0.5954
NFM	0.9746	0.1915	0.7352	0.5988
IPNN	0.9791	0.1759	0.7404	0.5945
DCN	0.9789	0.1814	0.7403	0.5944
FiBiNET	0.9787	0.1867	0.7405	0.5942
DeepFM	0.9789	0.1770	0.7402	0.5944
xDeepFM	0.9792	0.1889	0.7405	0.5940
AutoInt+	0.9786	0.1890	0.7406	0.5939
AFN+	0.9791	0.1824	0.7404	0.5945
DCN-V2	0.9802	0.1783	0.7411	0.5935
GDCN	0.9813	0.1602	0.7413	0.5935
DeepFM$_{FRNet}$	0.9818	0.1583	0.7418	0.5913
FRGCN(our)	0.9838	0.1513	0.7446	0.5906

number of layers in the MHSA, and the number of layers in the cross network
in the feature interaction layer.

Number of Attention Heads. Multi-head self-attention captures different types
of information through different attention heads, and captures patterns and relationships in the data more comprehensively through multiple attention heads.
In order to investigate the effect of the number of attention heads on the model
performance, this paper conducts a tuning experiment, keeping other parameters
fixed, and the experimental results are shown in Fig. 4. On the Frappe dataset,
the model performance first rises and then decreases. FRGCN has the best performance when the value of the number of attention heads on the Frappe dataset
is taken to be 4. The model performance on the Malware dataset shows an overall
increasing trend, and FRGCN performance reaches its best when the number of
heads takes the value of 8 in the set range of values. Comparing the two datasets,
the performance decreases with larger values of the number of heads, which may
be related to the fact that the Frappe dataset has a smaller number of features.
On the Frappe dataset, the model using fewer number of heads is sufficient to
capture the main relationships in the data and reduce the risk of overfitting.
The results therefore suggest that the number of attention heads does not take a
larger value for better model performance, and that the optimal number of heads
should be determined in conjunction with the characteristics of the dataset in
order to achieve better model performance.

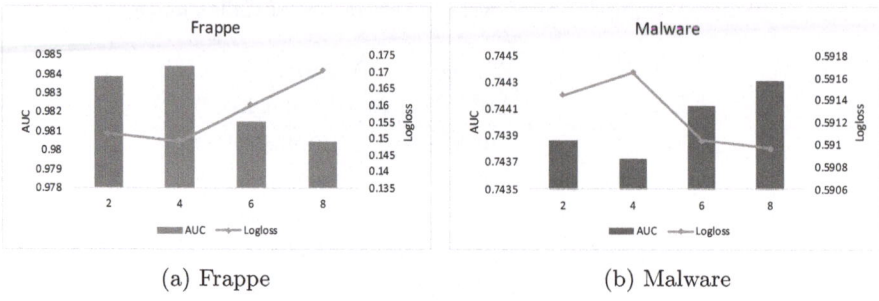

(a) Frappe   (b) Malware

Fig. 4. Number of Attention Heads.

Number of Attention Layers. By increasing the number of multi-headed self-attention layers, the model can learn more complex features and patterns. As the number of layers increases, the number of parameters of the model increases, which gives the model greater expressive power. In order to investigate the effect of the number of attention layers on the model performance, this paper conducts a tuning parameter experiment. Keeping the other parameters fixed, it can be seen from Fig. 5 that the model performance increases and then decreases on the Frappe and Malware datasets. FRGCN has the best performance when the number of attention layers is 2 on both datasets. The results suggest that when the number of layers is increased to a certain level, the model may become too complex and start to overfit on the training data, leading to a decrease in performance on the validation and test sets.

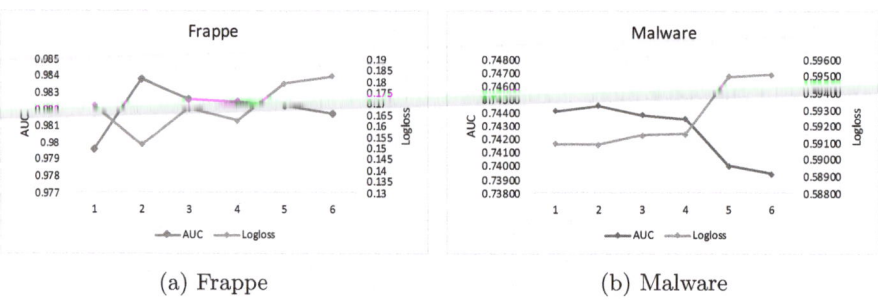

(a) Frappe   (b) Malware

Fig. 5. Number of Attention Layers.

Layers of Cross Network. The core function of a cross network is to capture complex nonlinear interactions between features. Through the cross layers, the model can model the higher-order interactions of the input features, thus capturing the potential relationships between the features. In order to investigate the effect of the number of layers of the cross network on the experimental results, this paper conducts a tuning experiment. Keeping other parameters fixed and setting the number of layers from 1 to 7, and the experimental results are shown in Fig. 6. It can be found that when the number of layers is set from less to more, the overall model performance shows an upward trend more stable.

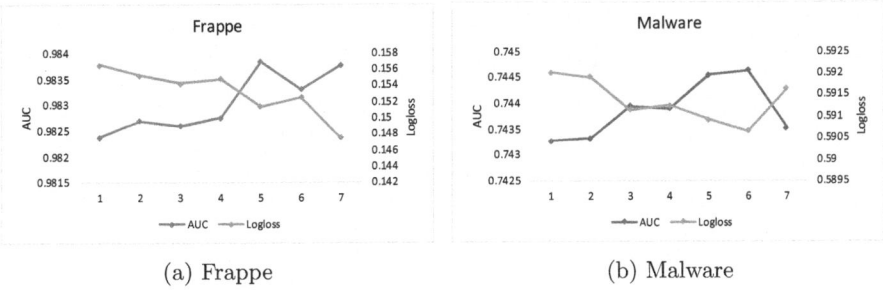

(a) Frappe   (b) Malware

Fig. 6. Number of Cross Network Layer.

Through the analysis of the experimental results, it can be learned that the number of heads and layers in the MHSA, as well as the number of layers of the cross-network in the feature interaction layer, have a certain impact on the performance of the FRGCN. When choosing these hyperparameters, the model performance and computational cost need to be carefully weighed in order to select the appropriate hyperparameters to obtain the best performance.

Ablation Experiments. In this paper, experiments are conducted on Frappe and Malware datasets to verify the effectiveness of each component in FRGCN. The FRGCN is set up as a basic model, and then keep the other parts unchanged to remove a component and observe the performance change, the results are shown in Table 3 shows.

Table 3. Performance of FRGCN removal related components.

Model	Frappe		Malware	
	AUC	Logloss	AUC	Logloss
BASE	0.9838	0.1514	0.7446	0.5906
MHSA removal	0.9829	0.1516	0.7436	0.5915
GCN removal	0.9823	0.1536	0.7439	0.5914
IEU$_C$ removal	0.9817	0.1564	0.7435	0.5916
FRNet removal	0.9816	0.1684	0.7426	0.5926
FRNet-A removal	0.9813	0.1602	0.7413	0.5935

MHSA Removal. On both datasets, compared to the BASE model, the model after removing the MHSA module shows a decrease in AUC of 0.09% and 0.13%, and an increase in Logloss values of 0.13% and 0.15%, respectively. This result validates the effectiveness of MHSA and shows that the addition of MHSA can realize the enhancement of feature representation and thus improve the model performance.

GCN Removal. After removing the gated cross network, only the DNN is retained at the feature interaction layer to perform implicit higher-order interactions on features. The experimental results show that the AUC of the model decreases by 0.15% and 0.09%, and the Logloss value increases by 1.45% and 0.13% on the Frappe and Malware datasets, respectively. This result proves the effectiveness of increasing GCN and shows that explicit higher-order feature interactions are very indispensable in click-through rate prediction models.

IEU_C Removal. After removing the IEU_C module, the FRNet-A layer uses only one IEU module for the information representation of the generated context. The experimental results show that the AUC of the model decreases by 0.21% and 0.15%, and the Logloss value increases by 3.30% and 0.17% on the Frappe and Malware datasets, respectively. This result demonstrates the importance of the IEU_C module to generate supplementary features to enrich the feature space.

FRNet Removal. Removing the FRNet module i.e. FRNet-A layer with only MHSA in action, we use it to verify the effectiveness of the feature representation of fused contextual information in the model. From the data in Table 3, it can be seen that the AUC of the model decreases by 0.22% and 0.26% on Frappe and Malware datasets, respectively, and the Logloss value increases by 11.22% and 0.34%, respectively. Therefore, feature refinement incorporating contextual information can effectively improve the expressive ability of the model, and the experiment proves its effectiveness.

FRNet-A Removal. By removing the FRNet-A layer, the model degenerates into a GDCN model (GDCN model that is not optimized using the embedding dimension). The experimental results show that the AUC and Logloss of the model on Frappe and Malware datasets have decreased and increased to a great extent, respectively. Thus, the effectiveness of the FRNet-A layer is demonstrated.

In summary, each component in FRGCN plays a vital role, in other words in, to some extent, illustrating the validity of the model proposed in this paper.

5   Conclusions

In this paper, we propose a click-through prediction model incorporating feature refinement enhancement and cross network, abbreviated as FRGCN, which improves on the DeepFM model by adding the FRNet-A layer after the embedding layer as a way to realize context-aware representation of features and perform attentional enhancement. In addition, a gated cross network is introduced at the feature interaction layer instead of the FM module to capture higher-order explicit feature interactions. Compared with the baseline model, FRGCN performs better on the Frappe and Malware datasets. However, some issues for continued improvement were identified during the experiments. For example, increasing the number of layers usually captures more complex feature interactions and thus improves the predictive performance of the model. However, an increase in the number of layers also leads to an increase in computational complexity and may require longer training time. In subsequent work, we will continue to explore how to reduce computational complexity while ensuring model performance. For example, we will introduce more lightweight network structures to reduce the model's parameter count and computational load.

References

1. Lei, L., Jia, Z., Dong, Y.: Advertising click-through rate prediction model based on an attention mechanism and a neural network. Mob. Inf. Syst. **2022**(1), 1474354 (2022)
2. Cheng, H.T., et al.: Wide & deep learning for recommender systems. In: Proceedings of the 1st Workshop on Deep Learning for Recommender Systems, pp. 7–10 (2016)
3. Zhu, J., et al.: Bars: towards open benchmarking for recommender systems. In: Proceedings of the 45th International ACM SIGIR Conference on Research and Development in Information Retrieval, pp. 2912–2923 (2022)
4. Song, W., et al.: Autoint: automatic feature interaction learning via self-attentive neural networks. In: Proceedings of the 28th ACM International Conference on Information and Knowledge Management, pp. 1161–1170 (2019)
5. Wang, R., et al.: Dcn v2: improved deep & cross network and practical lessons for web-scale learning to rank systems. Proc. Web Conf. **2021**, 1785–1797 (2021)
6. Wang, F., Gu, H., Li, D., Lu, T., Zhang, P., Gu, N.: Towards deeper, lighter and interpretable cross network for ctr prediction. In: Proceedings of the 32nd ACM International Conference on Information and Knowledge Management, pp. 2523–2533 (2023)
7. Richardson, M., Dominowska, E., Ragno, R.: Predicting clicks: estimating the click-through rate for new ads. In: Proceedings of the 16th International Conference on World Wide Web, pp. 521–530 (2007)
8. Rendle, S.: Factorization machines. In: 2010 IEEE International Conference on Data Mining, pp. 995–1000. IEEE (2010)
9. Juan, Y., Zhuang, Y., Chin, W.S., Lin, C.J.: Field-aware factorization machines for ctr prediction. In: Proceedings of the 10th ACM Conference on Recommender Systems, pp. 43–50 (2016)
10. Lu, W., Yu, Y., Chang, Y., Wang, Z., Li, C., Yuan, B.: A dual input-aware factorization machine for ctr prediction. In: Proceedings of the Twenty-Ninth International Conference on International Joint Conferences on Artificial Intelligence, pp. 3139–3145 (2021)
11. Yu, Y., Wang, Z., Yuan, B.: An input-aware factorization machine for sparse prediction. IJCA **I**, 1466–1472 (2019)
12. Guo, H., Tang, R., Ye, Y., Li, Z., He, X.: Deepfm: a factorization-machine based neural network for ctr prediction. arXiv preprint arXiv:1703.04247 (2017)
13. Lian, J., Zhou, X., Zhang, F., Chen, Z., Xie, X., Sun, G.: xdeepfm: combining explicit and implicit feature interactions for recommender systems. In: Proceedings of the 24th ACM SIGKDD International Conference on Knowledge Discovery & Data Mining, pp. 1754–1763 (2018)

14. Wang, R., Fu, B., Fu, G., Wang, M.: Deep & cross network for ad click predictions. In: Proceedings of the ADKDD'17, pp. 1–7 (2017)
15. Wang, F., Wang, Y., Li, D., Gu, H., Lu, T., Zhang, P., Gu, N.: Enhancing ctr prediction with context-aware feature representation learning. In: Proceedings of the 45th International ACM SIGIR Conference on Research and Development in Information Retrieval, pp. 343–352 (2022)
16. Xiao, J., Ye, H., He, X., Zhang, H., Wu, F., Chua, T.S.: Attentional factorization machines: Learning the weight of feature interactions via attention networks. arXiv preprint arXiv:1708.04617 (2017)
17. Huang, T., Zhang, Z., Zhang, J.: Fibinet: combining feature importance and bilinear feature interaction for click-through rate prediction. In: Proceedings of the 13th ACM Conference on Recommender Systems, pp. 169–177 (2019)
18. Li, Z., Cheng, W., Chen, Y., Chen, H., Wang, W.: Interpretable click-through rate prediction through hierarchical attention. In: Proceedings of the 13th International Conference on Web Search and Data Mining, pp. 313–321 (2020)
19. YANG Bin, LIANG Jing, Z.J., Mengci, Z.: Research on explainable click-through rate prediction model based on attention mechanism. Comput. Sci. **50**(05), pp. 12–20 (2023)
20. Baltrunas, L., Church, K., Karatzoglou, A., Oliver, N.: Frappe: understanding the usage and perception of mobile app recommendations in-the-wild. arXiv preprint arXiv:1505.03014 (2015)
21. Cheng, W., Shen, Y., Huang, L.: Adaptive factorization network: learning adaptive-order feature interactions. In: Proceedings of the AAAI Conference on Artificial Intelligence, vol. **34**, pp. 3609–3616 (2020)
22. He, X., Chua, T.S.: Neural factorization machines for sparse predictive analytics. In: Proceedings of the 40th International ACM SIGIR Conference on Research and Development in Information Retrieval, pp. 355–364 (2017)
23. Wang, Z., She, Q., Zhang, J.: Masknet: introducing feature-wise multiplication to ctr ranking models by instance-guided mask. arXiv preprint arXiv:2102.07619 (2021)
24. Pan, J., et al.: Field-weighted factorization machines for click-through rate prediction in display advertising. In: Proceedings of the 2018 World Wide Web Conference, pp. 1049–1357 (2018)
25. Qu, Y.: Product-based neural networks for user response prediction over multi-field categorical data. ACM Trans. Inf. Syst. (TOIS) **37**(1), 1–35 (2018)
26. Guo, H., Chen, B., Tang, R., Zhang, W., Li, Z., He, X.: An embedding learning framework for numerical features in ctr prediction. In: Proceedings of the 27th ACM SIGKDD Conference on Knowledge Discovery & Data Mining, pp. 2910–2918 (2021)

XcepSENet: An Intelligent Yoga Pose Classification System Based on Mediapipe

Lu Yong$^{(\boxtimes)}$, Ding Fusen, and Li Jiayun

Minzu University of China, Beijing 10000, China
{2006153,22302096,21210012}@muc.edu.cn

Abstract. Yoga, with a history spanning hundreds of years, is often referred to as a "treasure of the world." As global emphasis on health and fitness increases, yoga, which integrates physical, mental, and spiritual practices, has gained significant popularity. Correct yoga poses are crucial for achieving optimal results. Therefore, accurate recognition and classification of yoga poses are of great importance to practitioners.

This paper introduces a novel intelligent yoga pose classification system, XcepSENet, which combines the feature extraction capabilities of Mediapipe with an improved Xception model and the SE blocks of SENet. Our system estimates and classifies five major types of yoga poses with low latency, aiming to provide high-accuracy and low-latency classification to assist practitioners in correcting their poses, thereby enhancing safety and effectiveness.

Furthermore, in the Yoga dataset, the XcepSENet network is compared with three deep learning models—VGG16, InceptionV3, and MobileNetV2—evaluating metrics such as accuracy, precision, recall, and F1 score to draw conclusions, To prove that the model can provide feedback more timely and accurately to achieve higher training effects.

Keywords: MediaPipe · deep learning · classification · Xception · SENet

1 Introduction

Yoga, an ancient fitness practice that blends body and mind, originated in India and has gradually gained global popularity. With the increasing prevalence of yoga practice, the demand for accurate pose recognition is growing. Correct yoga poses are crucial for achieving its physical and mental health benefits, while incorrect poses can lead to injuries [1]. Traditional yoga learning methods rely on face-to-face instruction, which lacks real-time feedback and cannot meet modern society's demand for convenience. The development of artificial intelligence, particularly in machine vision and image processing, offers the potential to assist in yoga pose recognition and classification.

This paper aims to develop a deep learning-based yoga pose recognition system called XcepSENet. This system combines the efficient feature extraction capabilities of Mediapipe with the advanced convolutional neural network architecture Xception and the attention mechanism of SENet. Through this integrated approach, our system not

X. Pan et al. (Eds.): AIMS 2024, LNCS 15421, pp. 35–50, 2025.
https://doi.org/10.1007/978-3-031-77681-6_3

only improves pose recognition accuracy but also enhances the model's ability to handle complex poses, enabling yoga practitioners to receive instant pose correction feedback even in the absence of a coach [2–4].

The main contributions of this study include: Firstly, Utilizing Mediapipe as a feature extraction tool to extract key posture data of yoga practitioners in real-time. Secondly, Combining the Xception model with SENet's Squeeze-and-Excitation(SE)attention mechanism, and improving upon this basis to design a new network architecture, XcepSENet, to enhance the learning and representation capabilities of the network for yoga pose features. Finally, Conducting extensive tests on the Yoga dataset, which includes various yoga poses, to verify the significant improvement in recognition accuracy of XcepSENet compared to existing technologies.

2 Related Work

Pose detection, particularly in the field of human pose estimation, is a core problem in computer vision research. The evolution of this technology has witnessed a significant transition from initial basic image processing methods to modern deep learning applications. These advancements have not only driven the technology forward but also greatly enhanced the effectiveness and usability of pose detection in practical applications.

The development of deep learning has significantly propelled technological advancements in various fields, especially in image and video processing. Deep learning architectures, particularly convolutional neural networks (CNNs), have become central to computer vision tasks [5]. Since the early success of AlexNet, more complex architectures such as VGG networks, ResNet, and Xception have been proposed and applied to various visual recognition tasks [6–8]. Systems like OpenPose and AlphaPose have further advanced pose detection technology, providing real-time solutions for multi-person pose estimation [9, 10].

The development of network models has greatly promoted the application of yoga posture classification in the field of image processing. Jose J. [11] explored using convolutional neural networks and transfer learning to recognize different yoga poses, utilizing a dataset of 700 images of various yoga poses for feature extraction and classification through deep learning models. Vivek Anand Thoutam et al. [12] developed a mechanism for detecting yoga poses and providing real-time feedback using computer vision and machine learning techniques. By analyzing images or videos of individuals performing yoga poses, computer vision technology can identify the specific pose being executed, which is then evaluated and feedback is generated using deep learning models. T.Anuradha et al. [13] utilized deep learning techniques in conjunction with OpenCV and MediaPipe tools to recognize and analyze yoga poses. Byeon et al. [14] developed a pose recognition system based on various deep learning models to adapt to applications in different household environments, improving the accuracy and robustness of human pose recognition in complex home settings. Wang et al. [15], in a 2021 study, proposed a big data neural network model for yoga action recognition. This model leverages a complex neural network architecture to process and recognize a large volume of yoga action data, providing more precise feedback and improvement suggestions in yoga teaching and practice. A.D. Dobrzycki et al. [16] explored the application of contrastive language-image pretraining (CLIP) technology in human pose classification, particularly for yoga pose analysis. A. Bera et al. [17] established a benchmark analysis for fine-grained sports, yoga, and dance pose recognition, comparing various recognition techniques and methods to evaluate their effectiveness and accuracy in recognizing complex and subtle movements. K.A. Tanjaya et al. [18] studied the classification of Pilates poses using MediaPipe technology and convolutional neural networks (CNN), combined with transfer learning methods. S. Garg et al. [19] employed deep learning methods based on CNN and MediaPipe technology specifically for yoga pose classification. F.B. Ashraf et al. [20] introduced YoNet, a neural network model designed specifically for yoga pose classification. YoNet's optimized architecture enables effective recognition and classification of various yoga poses, enhancing both accuracy and efficiency.

Through literature research, it can be observed that existing methods either use relatively small datasets or still have room for improvement in terms of accuracy. Therefore, a Mediapipe-based intelligent yoga pose classification system is proposed to address these challenges.

3   Related Technology Introduction

This study includes Google's human pose detection library, MediaPipe, and various transfer learning architectures. The transfer learning models included in the study are VGG16, InceptionV3, and MobileNetV2. Deploying these models aims to compare our proposed model with existing technologies. The following sections will introduce MediaPipe and the various transfer learning architectures.

3.1   MediaPipe

MediaPipe is an open-source, cross-platform framework developed by Google for building machine learning pipelines in multimedia applications. This framework allows developers to quickly implement real-time processing and analysis of video, image, and audio using pre-built models and libraries. It has significant applications in face detection, gesture recognition, human pose estimation, object detection, and tracking. Figure 1 shows the results of MediaPipe on yoga and fitness poses. MediaPipe excels at handling real-time images and videos, enabling it to achieve better results with low latency.

For yoga pose detection, we can use MediaPipe's BlazePose model. BlazePose utilizes a detector and a tracker to detect human keypoints. The detector is used to find regions of interest in the image, while the tracker attempts to identify pose landmarks [2, 21]. BlazePose can recognize and track multiple keypoints, including those of the body, face, and hands, making it suitable for various complex poses and movements. BlazePose is capable of detecting 33 or more keypoints on the human body, covering the entire body, including the torso, limbs, and keypoints on the hands and face, as shown in Fig. 2.

Fig. 1. Results of Mediapipe on Yoga and Fitness Poses

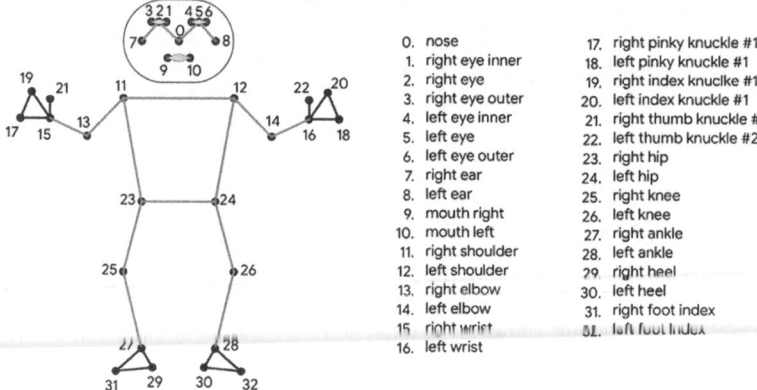

0.	nose	17.	right pinky knuckle #1
1.	right eye inner	18.	left pinky knuckle #1
2.	right eye	19.	right index knuclke #1
3.	right eye outer	20.	left index knuckle #1
4.	left eye inner	21.	right thumb knuckle #2
5.	left eye	22.	left thumb knuckle #2
6.	left eye outer	23.	right hip
7.	right ear	24.	left hip
8.	left ear	25.	right knee
9.	mouth right	26.	left knee
10.	mouth left	27.	right ankle
11.	right shoulder	28.	left ankle
12.	left shoulder	29.	right heel
13.	right elbow	30.	left heel
14.	left elbow	31.	right foot index
15.	right wrist	32.	left foot index
16.	left wrist		

Fig. 2. Coordinates of the 33 Key Points Detected by MediaPipe on the Human Body

3.2 Various Deep Learning Models

This paper discusses three deep learning models: VGG16, InceptionV3, and MobileNetV2. The following is a brief introduction to each of these models.

VGG16. VGG16 is a convolutional neural network architecture developed by Karen Simonyan and Andrew Zisserman from the Visual Geometry Group at the University of Oxford in 2014. The model performed exceptionally well in the ImageNet Challenge and is renowned for its 16-layer deep network structure, which includes 13 convolutional layers and 3 fully connected layers, as shown in Fig. 3. VGG16 employs multiple repeated 3×3 small convolutional kernels and 2×2 max-pooling layers, with approximately

138 million parameters in total. Despite the high number of parameters increasing computational demand, it endows the model with strong learning capabilities. The structure of VGG16 demonstrated the importance of network depth and the effectiveness of small convolutional kernels in enhancing feature learning accuracy. The model is typically pre-trained on the ImageNet dataset, enabling it to capture rich image features and making it suitable for various tasks.

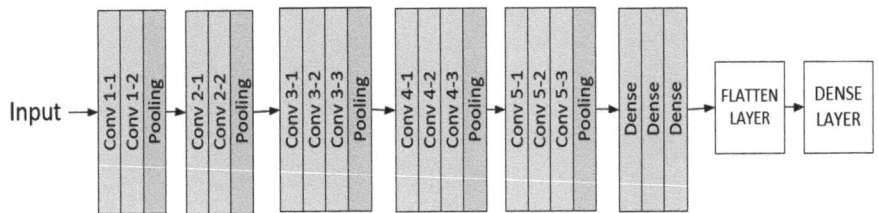

Fig. 3. VGG16 Network Model Architecture

InceptionV3. InceptionV3 is the third version of the Inception series introduced by Google in 2015 [22–24], as illustrated in Fig. 4. Building upon improvements from the previous versions, InceptionV3 aims to enhance recognition capability while reducing computational resource consumption. This version introduces the complex "Inception module," incorporating several technical innovations such as factorizing 5×5 convolutions into two 3×3 convolutions, using 1×3 and 3×1 convolutions to optimize efficiency, and adding auxiliary classifiers in the middle of the network to accelerate training and mitigate the vanishing gradient problem. Additionally, InceptionV3 improves training stability and efficiency through batch normalization and optimized grid reduction strategies. The model has approximately 23.8 million parameters, outperforming many deep networks by exhibiting excellent recognition accuracy and computational efficiency. InceptionV3 is typically pre-trained on the ImageNet dataset, and its structural design helps to reduce the risk of overfitting and improve generalization capabilities. However, the complexity of the model might limit its deployment in resource-constrained environments.

MobileNetV2. MobileNetV2 is a lightweight deep neural network introduced by Google in 2018, designed to improve visual recognition efficiency on mobile and edge devices, as illustrated in Fig. 5. This is the second generation of the MobileNet series [25, 26], addressing issues from the first generation such as the lack of residual connections and ineffective training of many Depthwise convolution kernels. MobileNetV2 introduces an inverted residual structure, using linear activation functions to optimize the dimensionality reduction process. It processes features through 1×1 Pointwise convolution for dimensionality increase, 3×3 Depthwise convolution, and another 1×1 Pointwise convolution for dimensionality reduction, followed by residual connections. This structure helps to reduce the model parameters to approximately 3.4 million, improving computational efficiency. Despite multiple optimizations, MobileNetV2 may still underperform in certain specific datasets or scenarios. The model is typically pre-trained on the ImageNet dataset.

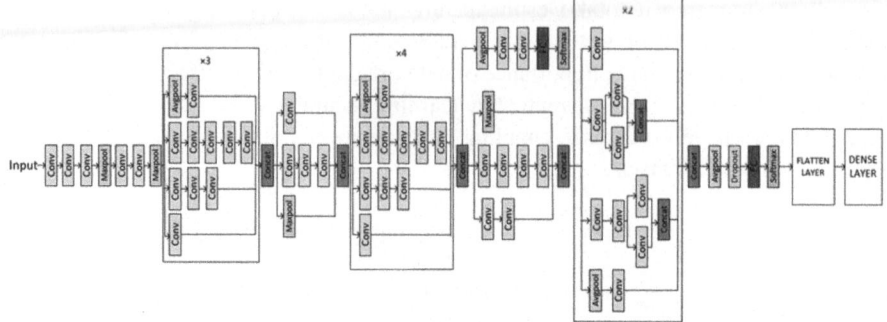

Fig. 4. InceptionV3 Network Model Architecture

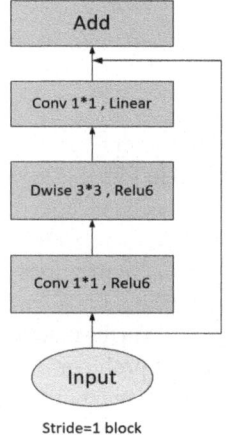

Fig. 5. Architecture of a Block in MobileNetV2

4 Proposed Model XcepSENet

This study proposes a custom-designed model, XcepSENet, for yoga pose classification, which can accurately and with low latency classify yoga postures. The experiment was conducted on the Yoga dataset.

4.1 DataSet

The dataset used in this experiment is a yoga pose dataset obtained from Kaggle, which is a type of public dataset [18, 27]. The dataset is divided into training and testing subdirectories, with each directory containing 5 subfolders corresponding to 5 types of yoga poses. These 5 yoga poses are Downward Dog (320 images), Goddess Pose (260 images), Tree Pose (229 images), Plank Pose (381 images), and Warrior Pose (361 images), totaling 1551 images. The training set contains 1081 images, and the test set contains 470 images. This dataset is a public dataset for yoga posture classification. It contains participants of different ages, skin colors and body shapes, and is evenly distributed in terms of gender to improve the generalization ability of the model.. Examples of each yoga pose are shown in Fig. 6.

Fig. 6. Downdog (a), Goddess (b), Plank (c), Tree (d), Warrior (e)

4.2 Data Preprocessing

Firstly, the images in the dataset are meticulously preprocessed: after reading the images, they are uniformly resized to 224×224 pixels to ensure consistency in subsequent processing. Using the MediaPipe tool, the images undergo skeletonization to accurately extract the 33 keypoint coordinates of the human body. These keypoints are then plotted on an all-black empty NumPy array, retaining only the keypoint information, thus generating a simplified image representing the human pose. To further process the images, their pixel values are divided by 255 to normalize them to a range of 0 to 1. This step helps to enhance the efficiency and effectiveness of the model training. The processed image data and their labels are stored in NumPy file format and saved in a newly created directory for quick loading and usage in the future.

Subsequently, image augmentation techniques are applied to the preprocessed training dataset. These techniques include rotation (rotation_range = 10 degrees), width shift (width_shift_range = 10%), height shift (height_shift_range = 10%), shear transformation (shear_range = 10%), zoom (zoom_range = 10%), and horizontal flip (horizontal_flip = True). The "nearest" fill mode (fill_mode = 'nearest') is used to handle blank areas caused by transformations. These image augmentation measures effectively increase the diversity of the data, enhance the model's ability to adapt to new scenarios, and reduce overfitting. The augmented training data is then used to train the XcepSENet model. During training, the model iteratively learns and optimizes its parameters to best recognize different human poses.

Finally, the preprocessed but unaugmented test dataset is fed into the trained XcepSENet model for final performance evaluation. This series of meticulous steps ensures the effective utilization of data and the efficiency of model training, with the ultimate goal of enhancing the model's accuracy and robustness in real-world applications.

4.3 Experiment with XcepSENet Model

The model is built on the Xception architecture and incorporates the Squeeze-and-Excitation (SE) attention mechanism from SENet, further enhancing feature capture and utilization [28]. Additionally, the model integrates various layers such as Conv2D, MaxPooling2D, Dropout, Dense, and Flatten to achieve precise classification for the five target categories. The structure of the model is illustrated in Fig. 7.

In the Xception model, depthwise separable convolution is primarily applied, which combines depthwise convolution and pointwise convolution in two steps. Depthwise convolution applies a separate convolutional filter to each input feature map channel. Unlike traditional convolution, which applies convolutional filters across all input channels, depthwise convolution convolves each input channel individually, thus reducing the number of parameters. For each input channel m, a $K \times K$ convolutional filter W_m (where W represents the weights of the depthwise convolution) is applied. This process can be expressed as:

$$D_{k,l,m} = \sum_{i=1}^{K} \sum_{j=1}^{K} I_{k+i,l+j,m} \cdot W_{i,j,m}$$

In this context, I represents the input feature map, D is the output feature map after depthwise convolution, (k, l) are the position indices on the output feature map, m is the channel index, and $W_{i,j,m}$ is the weight of the convolutional filter at position (i, j) in the m-th channel. After depthwise convolution, the output feature map retains its spatial dimensions, but the number of channels remains unchanged, with feature extraction occurring independently within each channel. Pointwise convolution, on the other hand, uses a 1×1 convolutional filter to convolve the output of the depthwise convolution, aiming to combine the features extracted across different channels. Pointwise convolution can be described as applying a full-depth 1×1 convolution at each position in D. This process can be expressed as:

$$P_{k,l,n} = \sum_{m=1}^{M} D_{k,l,m} \cdot V_{m,n} + B_n$$

In this context, P represents the output feature map after pointwise convolution, D is the output of the depthwise convolution, V is the weight of the pointwise convolution, B is the bias term, n is the channel index of the output feature map, and M is the number of channels in the input feature map. Pointwise convolution can change the number of channels in the feature map because the weights V of each 1×1 convolutional filter are multiplied by the corresponding positions of all channels in the output D from the depthwise convolution, and then summed over the channel dimension to produce a new feature map P. . This allows for the recombination and fusion of features generated by depthwise convolution. In depthwise separable convolution, the ReLU activation function is typically applied after each convolution step, meaning a ReLU activation follows both the depthwise and pointwise convolutions. This introduces non-linearity, enabling the neural network to learn and model more complex functions. In the batch normalization layer (Batch Normalization), this process can be expressed as:

$$\hat{x}_i = \frac{x_i - \mu_B}{\sqrt{\sigma_B^2 + \epsilon}}$$

$$y_i = \gamma \hat{x}_i + \beta = BN_{\gamma,\beta}(x_i)$$

In this context, x_i is the input value, μ_B is the mean of the batch, σ_B^2 is the variance of the batch, ϵ is a small constant added for numerical stability, γ and β are learnable parameters, y_i is the output value.

When using Xception as the base model, the model employs weights pre-trained on the ImageNet dataset to leverage the rich features already learned. To adapt the model to the new classification task, we removed the top layers of the Xception model (i.e., the portion after the global average pooling layer) and replaced them with a custom network layer structure. In the retained Xception model, the final 20 layers are set to a trainable state, allowing the weights of these layers to be adjusted during subsequent training to adapt to the new data features. This fine-tuning process ensures that the model can effectively learn the specific characteristics of the new classification task, improving its performance on the target dataset.

From the feature map output by the Xception model, the custom network layers begin with a Conv2D convolution layer configured with 64 filters, a kernel size of 3 × 3, and a ReLU activation function. This layer is used to further extract detailed features from the images. Following this is a BatchNormalization layer, which standardizes the activations from the previous layer, accelerating the training process and improving the model's convergence speed and stability. Next, a Squeeze-and-Excitation (SE) block is introduced. This mechanism adaptively recalibrates channel responses, enhancing key features and suppressing less important information, thereby improving the overall expressiveness of the model. After the SE block, the data flows through a MaxPooling2D layer with a 2 × 2 window, effectively reducing the size of the feature map and lowering computational load. A Dropout layer is then used, randomly dropping 50% of the neurons as an effective regularization strategy to help prevent overfitting. The Flatten layer then flattens the multidimensional output to prepare it for the fully connected layers. In the fully connected layers, the first is a Dense layer with 256 units, using the ReLU activation function. L2 regularization (with a regularization strength of 0.01) is applied to further control model complexity and prevent overfitting. Finally, the output layer is a Dense layer with 5 units, using the softmax activation function to output the predicted probabilities for each class, completing the model construction.

The entire model design leverages the powerful feature extraction capabilities of the pre-trained model while incorporating attention mechanisms and efficient training strategies. This combination enables the model to excel in multi-class image classification tasks, enhancing both accuracy and robustness.

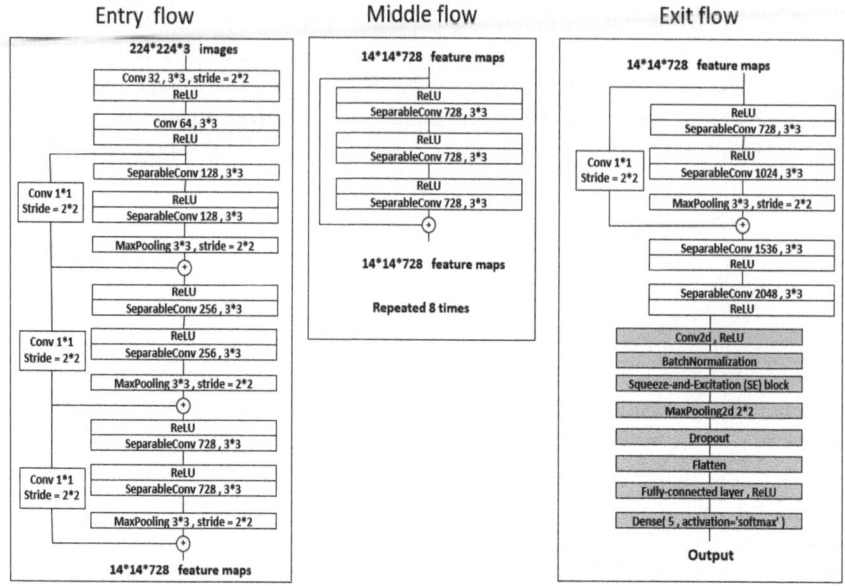

Fig. 7. XcepSENet Model Architecture

The Squeeze-and-Excitation (SE) block is an innovative mechanism designed to enhance the performance of convolutional neural networks (CNNs), particularly in strengthening channel attention. Its specific structure is shown in Fig. 8. This mechanism effectively enhances the network's feature representation ability by finely adjusting the importance of each channel. The Squeeze step compresses the spatial dimensions (height and width) through global average pooling, generating a single statistic for each channel. For a given input feature map U (assuming dimensions $H \times W \times C$, where C is the number of channels), the output z of the global average pooling for each channel C is calculated as follows:

$$z_c = \frac{1}{H \times W} \sum_{i=1}^{H} \sum_{j=1}^{W} U_{i,j,c}$$

In this context, $U_{i,j,c}$ is the value of the feature map U at position (i, j) in the C-th channel. The Excitation step involves a non-linear transformation and rescaling of the compressed signal using a learned transformation function g composed of two fully connected layers. First, the result z from the global average pooling is passed through a fully connected layer with weights W_1 and a ReLU activation function. Then, it goes through a second fully connected layer with weights W_2 and a Sigmoid activation function to generate the weight vector s. This process can be described as follows:

$$s = \sigma(g(z, W)) = \sigma(W_2 \delta(W_1 z))$$

Here, δ represents the ReLU activation function $\delta(x) = \max(0, x)$, and σ represents the Sigmoid activation function $\sigma(x) = \frac{1}{1+e^{-x}}$. W_1 is the weight matrix of the first fully connected layer, typically with dimensions $\frac{c}{r}$, where r 是 is the reduction ratio. W_2 is the weight matrix of the second fully connected layer with dimensions C. Finally, the generated weight vector s is used to rescale each channel of the original input feature map U:

$$\tilde{U}_{i,j,c} = s_c \cdot U_{i,j,c}$$

Here, $\tilde{U}$ is the rescaled feature map, s_c is the C-th element of the weight vector s. This process allows the network to perform adaptive feature recalibration, meaning that it learns to assign different levels of importance to each channel. This enhances the network's expressive power by emphasizing crucial features while suppressing less important ones.

Specifically, the operation process of the SE (Squeeze-and-Excitation) block can be divided into three main stages: Squeeze, Excitation, and Scale. First, in the Squeeze stage, the input feature map (usually a multi-dimensional data tensor produced by previous convolutional layers) is stored in the variable init, while confirming the position index of the channels in the data tensor. Then, Global Average Pooling (GlobalAveragePooling2D) is applied to this feature map, a process that summarizes the spatial information of each channel into a single scalar, achieving an efficient "squeeze" from the spatial dimension to the channel dimension. In the Excitation stage, the squeezed features are further transformed and learned through a series of fully connected layers combined with appropriate activation functions (the first fully connected layer uses the ReLU activation function, while the second fully connected layer uses the Sigmoid activation function), generating an attention vector that describes the importance of each channel. This attention vector accurately evaluates and reflects the contribution of each channel to the current learning task. Finally, in the Scale stage, the original input feature map is element-wise multiplied by the attention vector generated in the Excitation stage. The key to this step is to reweight each channel through this multiplication operation, thereby adjusting and optimizing the contribution of each channel in the network, ensuring that important channels are enhanced while less important channels are correspondingly suppressed. By integrating these three stages, the SE block significantly improves the network's responsiveness to important features, enhancing the overall performance of the model.

XcepSENet is implemented to process 224×224 pixel three-channel image inputs, optimized for a specific pose classification task. The model's output layer is customized according to different pose categories, ensuring effective recognition of each category. Through continuous parameter tuning, the model achieves optimal performance. The Adam optimizer is employed with a learning rate set at 0.0001, which helps smoothly and accurately update the network weights, thereby improving learning efficiency. The loss function used is categorical_crossentropy, which is well-suited for handling multi-class classification problems as it effectively amplifies the impact of prediction errors, forcing the model to focus more on correct classification. The model's training process lasted for 100 epochs, ensuring that the model could fully learn and adapt to the complex features of the training data. In the testing phase post-training, the model underwent a detailed evaluation, including the generation of a confusion matrix to visualize the model's performance across different categories. In the confusion matrix, the categories are labeled from 0 to 4, corresponding to five yoga poses: downdog, goddess, plank, tree,

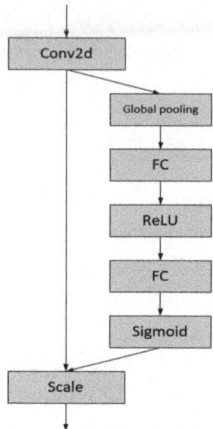

Fig. 8. SE Block

and warrior. Additionally, the overall performance of the model was comprehensively evaluated through accuracy, precision, recall, and F1 score, providing a comparative assessment of the performance of four different models from multiple perspectives.

5   Results and Discussion

A paper During the 100 training epochs using the XcepSENet model, we observed significant stability and superiority in the trends of accuracy and loss function, as illustrated in Fig. 9. These curve charts provide a visual representation of the model's performance throughout the training process. After the initial 10 epochs, the accuracy quickly rose above 95% and maintained this high level consistently, indicating that the model had effectively learned to distinguish between different yoga poses. This early surge in accuracy demonstrates the appropriateness of the model's optimization settings and its excellent learning efficiency. Similarly, the loss function curve offers insights from another perspective. In the initial stages of training, the curve shows a significant decrease, highlighting the model's effectiveness in reducing prediction errors. Notably, from the 80th epoch onwards, the loss value stabilized around 0.2, suggesting that the model had reached a stable state of loss minimization. This steady low loss level further confirms the robustness and generalization capability of the model. Overall, the XcepSENet model exhibited remarkable stability and reliability, with no signs of overfitting.

Subsequently, we analyzed the XcepSENet model using a confusion matrix, as shown in Fig. 10. This confusion matrix clearly reveals the model's exceptional performance in the classification task of five yoga poses, with minimal errors and extremely high accuracy. From the confusion matrix, we can see that the prediction accuracy for the downdog pose reached 97%, for the goddess pose it reached 96.3%, for the plank pose it achieved 99%, for the tree pose it reached 95.8%, and for the warrior pose it achieved a perfect 100%.

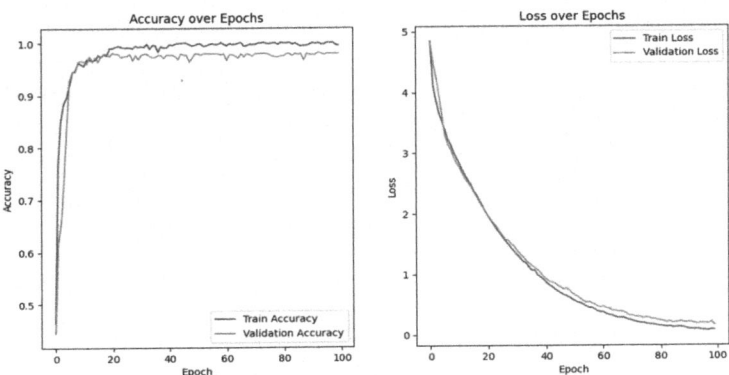

Fig. 9. Accuracy and Loss Graphs for the XcepSENet

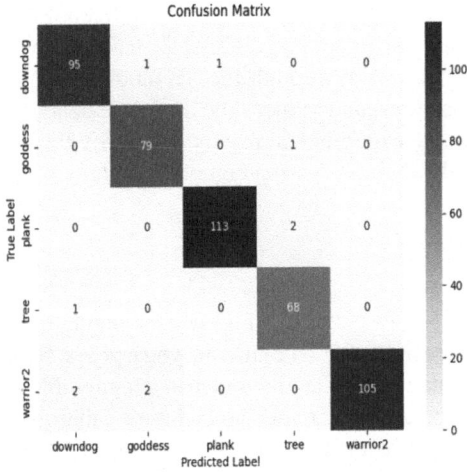

Fig. 10. XcepSENet Confusion Matrix on Test Set

In a study conducted on the Yoga dataset, the XcepSENet model was compared with three transfer learning models and the YogaConvo2d model proposed by Shubham Garg et al. in 2023. As shown in Table 1, the XcepSENet model significantly outperformed the other models across multiple performance metrics, including accuracy, precision, recall, and F1 score. These results underscore the efficiency and accuracy of the XcepSENet model in handling the Yoga pose recognition task.

Although VGG16 performs well in image classification tasks, its large number of parameters and complex calculations limit its performance in real-time applications. InceptionV3 effectively captures different signal features through its unique multi-branch structure (Inception module), and its efficiency is improved compared to VGG16, and the number of parameters is more reasonable. However, due to the complex model structure, the inference speed of InceptionV3 in real-time application scenarios is still limited. MobileNetV2 greatly reduces the calculation time through lightweight design,

Table 1. Accuracy comparison statistics of various deep learning models.

Model Names	Accuracy		Precision	Recall	F-1 Score
	Train	Test			
MobileNetV2	100	96.60	0.97	0.97	0.97
VGG16	96.53	96.86	0.97	0.97	0.97
InceptionV3	90.67	94.39	0.95	0.94	0.94
YogaConvo2d	99.35	97.09	0.97	0.97	0.97
XcepSENet	100	98.09	0.98	0.98	0.98

which is especially suitable for mobile devices. However, when processing complex postures, the performance of MobileNetV2 may be reduced because its network is shallow and cannot fully capture complex features. In contrast, XcepSENet not only inherits the advantages of InceptionV3 in processing multi-scale features, but also further optimizes the channel attention mechanism through the SE module, improves the classification accuracy of complex postures, and reduces the inference delay, so it performs better in real-time applications. The experimental results also verify this advantage. XcepSENet performs extremely well when processing complex postures.

6 Conclusion

Human pose detection has always been a highly challenging research topic in the field of computer vision, especially for recognizing yoga poses. This task is not only an important branch of human pose detection but also a highly difficult research direction. In this work, we propose a new network architecture called XcepSENet, which uses MediaPipe as a feature extractor. By integrating the deep learning capabilities of the Xception architecture with the attention mechanism in SENet, this approach effectively enhances the accuracy and efficiency of yoga pose recognition. The model achieves high-precision classification of common yoga poses, excelling particularly in the recognition of complex poses. This is of great significance for yoga practitioners, as correct postures are crucial for preventing injuries and maximizing the benefits of yoga practice.

The network can accurately classify yoga postures, and its application prospects in the future are very broad. In fact, the real-time nature of the network is not limited to yoga, but can also be applied to more fields. Real-time video analysis technology can provide personalized training guidance based on the user's real-time performance. By capturing the user's movement posture by the camera and comparing it with the standard movement, the system achieves accurate movement detection and correction. In addition, this technology can also be combined with the health system to monitor health conditions such as exercise monitoring intensity and heart rate, and issue alarms in time when abnormal behavior is found. In high-level competitive sports, real-time video analysis technology is integrated with virtual reality (VR) and augmented reality (AR) technology, and real-time video analysis further enhances the immersion and interactivity of the sports experience. There is still much work to be done in the field of human pose detection.

References

1. Ross, A., Thomas, S.: The health benefits of yoga and exercise: a review of comparison studies. J. Altern. Complement. Med. **16**(1), 3–12 (2010)
2. Lugaresi, C., Tang, J., Nash, H., et al.: Mediapipe: a framework for building perception pipelines. arXiv preprint arXiv:1906.08172 (2019)
3. Chollet, F.: Xception: deep learning with depthwise separable convolutions. In: Proceedings of the IEEE Conference on Computer Vision and Pattern Recognition, pp. 1251–1258 (2017)
4. Hu, J., Shen, L., Sun, G.: Squeeze-and-excitation networks. In: Proceedings of the IEEE Conference on Computer Vision and Pattern Recognition, pp. 7132–7141 (2018)
5. LeCun, Y., Bottou, L., Bengio, Y., et al.: Gradient-based learning applied to document recognition. Proc. IEEE **86**(11), 2278–2324 (1998)
6. Krizhevsky, A., Sutskever, I., Hinton, G.E.: Imagenet classification with deep convolutional neural networks. Adv. Neural Inf. Process. Syst. **25** (2012)
7. Simonyan, K., Zisserman, A.: Very deep convolutional networks for large-scale image recognition. arXiv preprint arXiv:1409.1556 (2014)
8. He, K., Zhang, X., Ren, S., et al.: Deep residual learning for image recognition. In: Proceedings of the IEEE Conference on Computer Vision and Pattern Recognition, pp. 770–778 (2016)
9. Cao, Z., Simon, T., Wei, S.E., et al.: Realtime multi-person 2D pose estimation using part affinity fields. In: Proceedings of the IEEE Conference on Computer Vision and Pattern Recognition, pp. 7291–7299 (2017)
10. Fang, H.S., Xie, S., Tai, Y.W., et al.: RMPE: regional multi-person pose estimation. In: Proceedings of the IEEE International Conference on Computer Vision, pp. 2334–2343 (2017)
11. Jose, J., Shailesh, S.: Yoga asana identification: a deep learning approach. In: IOP Conference Series: Materials Science and Engineering, vol. 1110(1), p. 012002. IOP Publishing (2021)
12. Thoutam, V.A., Srivastava, A., Badal, T., et al.: Yoga pose estimation and feedback generation using deep learning. Comput. Intell. Neurosci. **2022** (2022)
13. Anuradha, T., Krishnamoorthy, N., Kumar, C.S.P., et al.: A method for specifying yoga poses based on deep learning, utilizing OpenCV and media pipe technologies. Scalable Comput. Pract. Experience **25**(2), 739–750 (2024)
14. Byeon, Y.H., Lee, J.Y., Kim, D.H., et al.: Posture recognition using ensemble deep models under various home environments. Appl. Sci. **10**(4), 1287 (2020)
15. Wang, H.: Neural network-oriented big data model for yoga movement recognition. Comput. Intell. Neurosci. **2021**, 1–10 (2021)
16. Dobrzycki, A.D., Bernardos, A.M., Bergesio, L., et al.: Exploring the use of contrastive language-image pre-training for human posture classification: insights from yoga pose analysis. Mathematics **12**(1), 76 (2023)
17. Bera, A., Nasipuri, M., Krejcar, O., et al.: Fine-grained sports, yoga, and dance postures recognition: a benchmark analysis. IEEE Trans. Instrum. Measur. (2023)
18. Tanjaya, K.A., Naufal, M.F., Arwoko, H.: Pilates pose classification using mediapipe and convolutional neural networks with transfer learning. Jurnal Ilmiah Teknik Elektro Komputer dan Informatika (JITEKI) **9**(2), 212–222 (2023)
19. Garg, S., Saxena, A., Gupta, R.: Yoga pose classification: a CNN and mediapipe inspired deep learning approach for real-world application. J. Ambient Intell. Humaniz Comput., 1–12 (2022)

20. Ashraf, F.B., Islam, M.U., Kabir, M.R., et al.: YoNet: a neural network for yoga pose classification. SN Comput. Sci. **4**(2), 198 (2023)
21. Bazarevsky, V., Grishchenko, I., Raveendran, K., et al.: BlazePose: on-device real-time body pose tracking. arXiv preprint arXiv:2006.10204 (2020)
22. Szegedy, C., Liu, W., Jia, Y., et al.: Going deeper with convolutions. In: Proceedings of the IEEE Conference on Computer Vision and Pattern Recognition, pp. 1–9 (2015)
23. Ioffe, S., Szegedy, C.: Batch normalization: accelerating deep network training by reducing internal covariate shift. In: International Conference on Machine Learning. PMLR, pp. 448–456 (2015)
24. Szegedy, C., Vanhoucke, V., Ioffe, S., et al.: Rethinking the inception architecture for computer vision. In: Proceedings of the IEEE Conference on Computer Vision and Pattern Recognition, pp. 2818–2826 (2016)
25. Howard, A.G., Zhu, M., Chen, B., et al.: MobileNets: efficient convolutional neural networks for mobile vision applications. arXiv preprint arXiv:1704.04861 (2017)
26. Sandler, M., Howard, A., Zhu, M., et al.: MobileNetV2: inverted residuals and linear bottlenecks. In: Proceedings of the IEEE Conference on Computer Vision and Pattern Recognition, pp. 4510–4520 (2018)
27. Wells, C., Kolt, G.S., Bialocerkowski, A.: Defining pilates exercise: a systematic review. Complement. Ther. Med. **20**(4), 253–262 (2012)
28. Cheng, D., Meng, G., Cheng, G., et al.: SeNet: structured edge network for sea–land segmentation. IEEE Geosci. Remote Sens. Lett. **14**(2), 247–251 (2016)

Arg-T5: A Multi-perspective Argument Generation Method Based on Debate Topic

Zijian Wang, Mingjie Han, and Ting Jin(⊠)

School of Computer Science and Technology, Hainan University, Haikou 570228, China
jinting@hainanu.edu.cn

Abstract. This paper introduces an innovative approach to multi-perspective argument generation in the context of debate topics. Traditional text generation models, such as T5, often fall short in producing diverse arguments, leading to a lack of depth and diversity in debate simulations. To address this, we developed a method integrating perspective features into the dataset and leveraging the pre-trained Mengzi-T5 model to generate compelling arguments from multiple perspectives. Our method which is named Arg-T5, enhances the diversity of generated arguments and maintains relevance and persuasiveness. Through extensive experiments and comparisons with other models, including Mengzi-T5, Chat-GLM, and GPT-2, we demonstrate the superior performance of our approach. The outcomes underscore a notable enhancement in argument diversity, addressing a pivotal challenge within computational argumentation. Our work contributes to advancing text generation and computational argumentation, offering a new solution for generating rich and varied debate content.

Keywords: Argument Generation · Multi-perspective Generation · Pretrained Model

1 Introduction

Argumentation [1, 2] is a fundamental means for humans to express viewpoints, conduct reasoning, and persuade others, encompassing multiple disciplines such as linguistics, logic, and rhetoric. In recent years, the study of argumentation has attracted the attention of computational linguists, giving rise to a new field of research known as Computational Argumentation [3]. In this field, text generation technology is particularly crucial, as it can enrich the content of debates and enhance the quality and efficiency of debates.

However, traditional text generation models, exemplified by T5 [4], often lack consideration of the diversity of arguments. Especially when facing certain debate topics, the arguments generated by the model tend to be singular and fail to fully cover different perspectives, with multiple arguments prone to repetition. Moreover, the existing datasets still lack diversity, preventing the model from learning and generating from multiple perspectives during training. Generating arguments with multiple perspectives and depth to support or refute specific debate topics remains a challenge.

X. Pan et al. (Eds.): AIMS 2024, LNCS 15421, pp. 51–62, 2025.
https://doi.org/10.1007/978-3-031-77681-6_4

This paper proposes a multi-perspective argument generation method based on debate topics. This method can generate diverse and in-depth arguments from different perspectives. Our study first analyzes the debate topic to determine possible argument perspectives and then introduces additional perspective features to the dataset. Based on this, we have constructed a text generation model, named Arg-T5, which is based on the pre-trained model Mengzi-T5 [5], which can automatically generate five persuasive and diverse arguments according to the debate topic and preset perspectives. In the experimental section, we will verify the effectiveness of our method through a series of experiments. The results show that compared with existing text generation methods, our method performs better and significantly improves the diversity of arguments.

Through the research in this paper, we hope to provide a new perspective and method for the fields of computational argumentation and text generation, promoting the development and application of related technologies.

The main contributions of our work are as follows:

- Manual annotation of the CCAC2023 dataset, introducing additional perspective features.
- Training the model for semantic relevance using the CCAC2023 dataset and combining prompt finetuning to transfer to downstream argument generation tasks.
- The proposed model Arg-T5 can be directly used for multi-perspective argument generation, requiring only the debate topic as input without any other annotations.
- Comparative experiments with multiple generative language models have proven the excellent performance of the model proposed in this paper.

2 Related Work

Traditional rule-based text generation methods [6–8] rely on predefined rules to generate text or use statistical models to create symbolic representations of words, which are then combined to complete the generation task. The main advantage of these methods is the ability to directly control the generated text, but they require substantial manual effort to define and maintain the rules, and the resulting text often lacks creativity and diversity.

In recent years, deep neural networks have achieved encouraging progress in an increasing number of fields. Text generation methods have gradually shifted from traditional rule-based and template-based approaches to data-driven neural network methods, with deep neural network-based text generation methods becoming the mainstream. The primary advantages of deep neural network-based methods lie in their automation and flexibility. Since these methods can automatically learn how to generate text from data, they can avoid the need for extensive human resources. Furthermore, because these methods can learn from large amounts of real text, the generated text often exhibits high quality and authenticity. Recurrent Neural Networks (RNNs) [9] are designed to model sequential information, allowing contextual information to be passed through the network so that relevant outputs from previous time steps can be applied to the current time step's operations. Long Short-Term Memory (LSTM) networks [10] add memory cells to RNNs, enabling them to retain information over longer periods. This helps to address the issue of long-term dependencies in text and the vanishing gradient problem in RNNs. Similar variants include Gated Recurrent Units (GRUs) [11], which are also designed for sequential text data.

In recent developments, models based on the attention mechanism have also been widely applied in the field of text generation. The most notable example is the Transformer model [12], which relies entirely on the self-attention mechanism to capture dependencies between different positions in the input sequence. Unlike traditional RNNs and LSTMs, the Transformer does not depend on sequential information during encoding and decoding. Instead, it models the relationships between all elements in the sequence in a global manner. This feature allows the Transformer to excel in handling long sequences of text, avoiding the long-term dependency issues and vanishing gradient problems associated with RNNs and LSTMs.

Building on this, pre-trained generative language models such as GPT-2 [13], T5, and BART [14] have significantly advanced the field of text generation. Autoregressive models, such as the GPT series, have demonstrated strong performance in generative tasks by predicting the subsequent text word by word, based on the preceding context, thereby producing high-quality natural language text. The T5 model combines the strengths of both autoencoding and autoregressive approaches by introducing task-specific templates within the encoder-decoder architecture, allowing it to handle various natural language processing tasks uniformly. During the inference phase, it generates complete sentences word by word from left to right using beam search (BS) [15]. Those models are pre-trained on large-scale text corpora and then fine-tuned on specific tasks, enabling them to adapt to different text generation tasks. These models generate more natural and coherent text by stacking multiple layers of Transformers and leveraging extensive contextual information. The pre-training and fine-tuning paradigm enables generative models to possess rich linguistic knowledge while effectively adapting to the requirements of specific tasks.

3   Method

In this study, we have completed the annotation of additional features for the dataset, and then we trained the data using the Mengzi-T5 model, ultimately achieving multi-perspective Chinese argument generation. Specifically, we organized a large amount of data, added perspective features to the data through manual annotation, and then fine-tuned the pre-trained language model Mengzi-T5 with a specialized argument generation pre-training method. Subsequently, the improved model Arg-T5 was deployed to generate five arguments that align with a given debate topic. During the generation phase, with the prompt fine-tuning techniques and leveraging the capabilities of the language model, our model can generate a diverse set of arguments from five different perspectives.

3.1   Argument Classification

To address the issue that traditional generative models cannot generate arguments from multiple perspectives and suffer from repetition in the arguments they generate, our study employs a multi-perspective argument classification method.

Our research utilizes analytical tools to examine the dataset, categorizing arguments into eight major classes: definition, impact, method, background, refutation, exemplification, comparison, and unknown. The criteria for classification are as follows:

1. *Definition* refers to arguments that explain and introduce certain terms within the debate topic.
2. *Impact* pertains to the effects of the debate topic, which can generally refer to advantages or disadvantages.
3. *Method* refers to the debater's advocacy arguments, typically using phrases like "we should" or "we need to."
4. *Background* refers to the social and developmental context in which the debate topic is situated.
5. *Refutation* is the counter-argument directed towards the opposing debater, often using terms like "the opposing debater."
6. *Exemplification* includes specific examples within the argument, such as "high school seniors, the Green Gang."
7. *Comparison* is the act of contrasting different viewpoints to illustrate the correctness of one's own argument.
8. *Unknown* refers to argument that do not fit into any of the above categories, or those of poor quality without clearly expressing the debater's viewpoint. Arguments should be closely related to the debate topic; if a debater's argument strays off-topic, it is also considered unclassified.

These categories of arguments are not related to the specific name of the debate topic and will appear in any debate competition. Moreover, it is acceptable for an argument to belong to two or more categories simultaneously. Subsequently, we invited seven scholars in the field of Natural Language Processing to spend ten days categorizing each argument of every debate topic into one or more categories. They exchanged their classification results with other researchers, engaging in mutual review, discussion, and

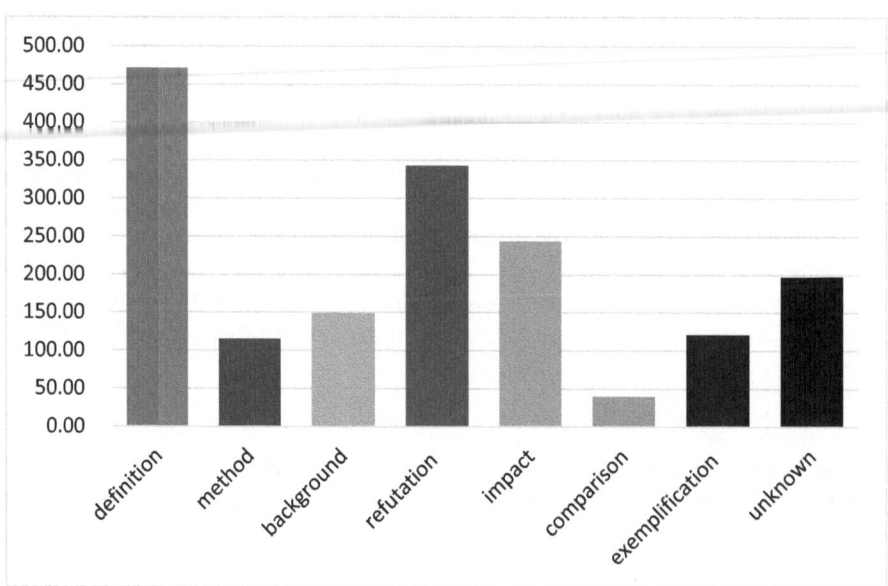

Fig. 1. Argument Classification Results

revision. Ultimately, all classification outcomes were submitted to an expert in the NLP field for final confirmation, yielding our definitive set of categorized results. Given the multitude of combinations possible with multiple categories, we will only present the classification results for single categories. The classification results for single categories are illustrated in Fig. 1.

Table 1. The classification of some arguments

Argument	Perspective
在讨论辩题之前, 首先跟大家明确几个概念, 佛系是指看淡一切、怎样都好的生活方式和人生态度。(Before delving into the debate topic, let's first clarify a few concepts with everyone: "Buddhist style" refers to a lifestyle and attitude towards life that is indifferent to everything and accepts any outcome with equanimity.)	Definition
而在我方看来这个成长是什么? 我方认为佛系这个标签挂到青年之上身上之后, 它会丢失掉一些生活机会。(But in our view, what is this growth? We believe that once the label "Buddhist-style" is attached to the youth, it will cause the loss of some life opportunities.)	Impact
二来在心态上不要拥抱佛系标签成为你的习惯, 你彻底成佛, 你就不在人世。(Secondly, do not embrace the "Buddhist-style" label as a habit in your mindset; if you become completely Buddha-like, you would no longer be of this world.)	Method
第二个那对方告诉我们, 那哪怕我不主动好了, 社会有这么多压力, 逼着我我肯定会往前走的, 我不得不成长。(The second point is that our opponents have conveyed to us that even if I don't take the initiative, the pressures of society are so great that they will inevitably push me forward, and I will have no choice but to grow.)	Background
而今天我被贴上这个标签的时候, 首先不一定达到自我认同, 对方同学首先是认了这一件事情。(Today, when I am labeled, I do not necessarily achieve self-identification; the classmates on the other side first acknowledge this fact.)	Refutation
如果高中三年敢于拼三年, 最后看到我自己物理的极限在哪里, 我不管成与败, 这个时候我才可以说我努力过, 所以我才敢说我至少成长不管成与败, 如果成功了, 我成绩提升了, 如果失败过至少奋斗过, 心智坚韧了。(If I dare to work hard for three years during high school, and finally see where my limits are, regardless of success or failure, it is then that I can say I have strived. Therefore, I dare to say that I have grown at least, regardless of success or failure. If I succeed, my grades will improve; if I fail, at least I have fought, and my mind has become resilient.)	Exemplification

(*continued*)

Table 1. (*continued*)

Argument	Perspective
我把你当成一个脆弱稚嫩幼小的需要我呵护的学生, 来保护你所以这个社会不是没有温情, 它可以容许你的退缩, 但这绝对不是成长。(I regard you as a fragile, tender, and young student in need of my care and protection, so this society is not devoid of warmth; it can allow for your retreat. However, this is by no means growth.)	Comparison
谢谢主席, 各位好, 对方在这边一直告诉我们佛系标签是一个很中性的词, 但是不要忘记中性的词落在不同的地方的时候会有不同的诠释意义。(Thank you, Mr. Chairman and distinguished participants. Our opponents have been insisting that the term "Buddhist-style" is a neutral word, but let's not forget that a neutral term can take on different interpretations and meanings when placed in different contexts.)	Definition and Refutation

Taking the debate topic "The label Buddhist-style is more harmful than beneficial to growth" as an example, the classification of some arguments is shown in Table 1.

3.2 Multi-perspective Argument Generation Pre-training

After obtaining the classification results of arguments, our study adds perspective information to the dataset and sends it to the Mengzi-T5 model for training. Specifically, the format of the template is as follows:

"Topic: { }. Perspective: { }."

Where the first { } is filled with the debate topic, and the second { } is filled with the perspective category of the argument.

The model framework is visually depicted in Fig. 2. During training, corresponding perspective words are added according to the argument's category. During prediction, five types of perspective words are selected to generate arguments from five different perspectives. By training with the CCAC2023 dataset that includes perspective features, we have obtained a model specifically designed for argument generation named Arg-T5.

3.3 Multi-perspective Argument Generation

During prediction, our study employs an input method that involves instruction fine-tuning. Typically, instruction fine-tuning is performed directly on pre-trained models without using downstream task datasets, but our study chooses to attempt both methods simultaneously. Prompt fine-tuning enables few-shot/zero-shot learning without modifying the model parameters. It makes model predictions without parameter updates by selecting some samples from the training set as task prompts or by providing Positive/Negative Examples, aiming to tap into the knowledge inherent in language models. After instruction fine-tuning, large language models can demonstrate a strong ability to follow instructions. As shown in Fig. 3, we have customized prompt templates for the argument generation task, including task definition and an example of input and output.

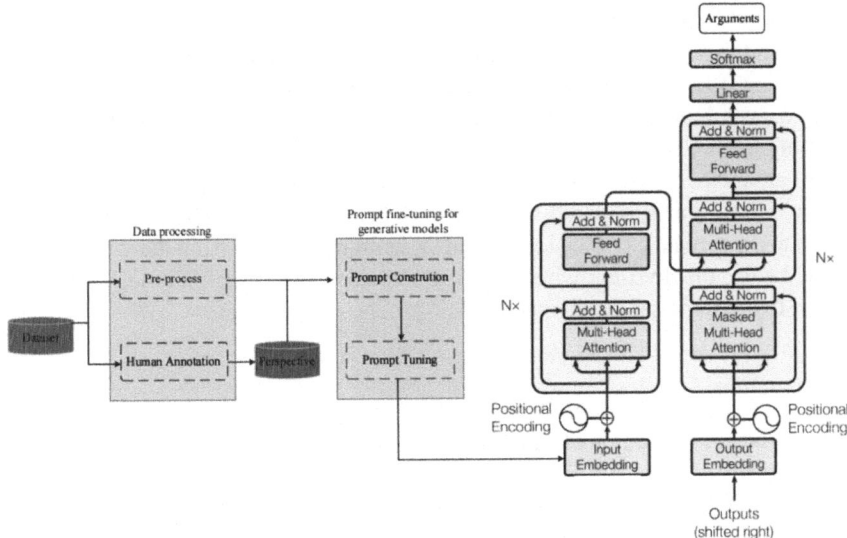

Fig. 2. Illustration of our proposed method

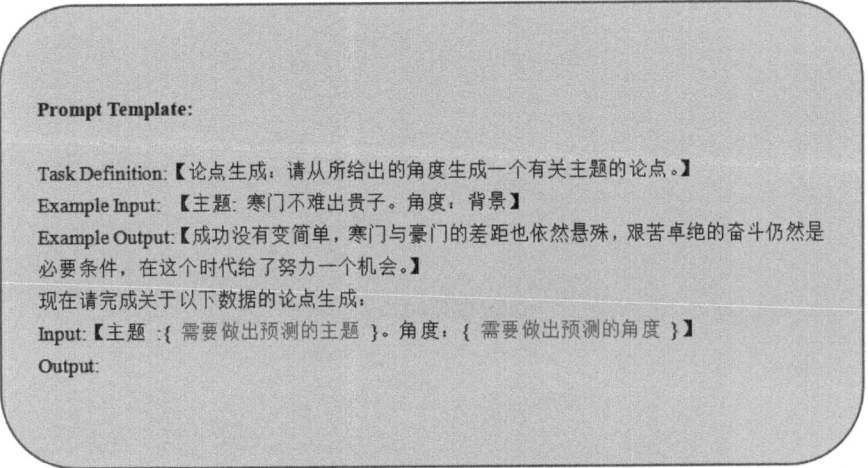

Fig. 3. Prompt finetuning template for argument generation

4 Experiments and Result Analysis

4.1 Dataset

In this paper, the model is trained using the CCAC2023 training set, which originates from nearly 700 renowned Chinese debate competitions held between 2007 and 2021. Transcripts of segments and monologues from each debate have been obtained through speech-to-text transcription and subsequent manual verification. Monologue texts are chunked based on punctuation such as periods and question marks, and then annotated by raters to identify arguments. Each argumentative sentence corresponds to the proposition of the current debate, thereby generating debate-argument data pairs.

The dataset includes 33 debate topics, with a total of 3,455 arguments, averaging 104.70 arguments per debate topic, and each topic having approximately 59 to 154 standard arguments. The dataset is divided into a training set, validation set, and test set based on debate topics, with a division ratio of 8:1:1. To prevent the model from being exposed to the semantics of the test set during training, debates from the same event are grouped before the division; when dividing, debates from the same group will only be assigned to the same set simultaneously.

4.2 Evaluation Metrics

For the argument generation task, our study employ the following metrics to assess the quality of generated texts: ROUGE-1, ROUGE-2, and ROUGE-L, which are calculated based on single words, consecutive 2 words, and the longest common subsequence, respectively. The method for calculating the final score is as follows:

$$S_m(rouge1) = \sum_{i=1}^{5} \sum_{n=1}^{N_m} \text{rouge1}\left(\text{Pred}_{(m,i)}, \text{Target}_{(m,n)}\right) \bigg/ 5 * \sum_{m=1}^{M} N_m \quad (1)$$

$$S(rouge1) = \sum_{m=1}^{M} S_m \bigg/ M \quad (2)$$

$$S_m(rouge2) = \sum_{i=1}^{5} \sum_{n=1}^{N_m} \text{rouge2}\left(\text{Pred}_{(m,i)}, \text{Target}_{(m,n)}\right) \bigg/ 5 * \sum_{m=1}^{M} N_m \quad (3)$$

$$S(rouge2) = \sum_{m=1}^{M} S_m \bigg/ M \quad (4)$$

$$S_m(rougeL) = \sum_{i=1}^{5} \sum_{n=1}^{N_m} \text{rougeL}\left(\text{Pred}_{(m,i)}, \text{Target}_{(m,n)}\right) \bigg/ 5 * \sum_{m=1}^{M} N_m \quad (5)$$

$$S(rougeL) = \sum_{m=1}^{M} S_m \bigg/ M \quad (6)$$

In the given context, M refers to the number of debate topics, N_m refers to the number of standard arguments for the m-th debate topic, S_m refers to the score for the m-th debate topic, and S refers to the total score. Pred(m,i) denotes the i-th predicted argument generated for the m-th debate topic, and Target(m,n) denotes the n-th standard argument for the m-th debate topic. Rouge1() refers to the ROUGE-1 calculation method. Rouge2() refers to the ROUGE-2 calculation method. RougeL() refers to the ROUGE-L calculation method.

It can be observed from the formulas above that the score obtained for the arguments generated by the model for each debate topic is the average Rouge-1, Rouge-2, and Rouge-L score between the predicted argument and the standard arguments.

4.3   Comparison with Other Methods

Several common text generation models were selected for comparative experiments in our study. The outputs can be seen in Table 2.

- Mengzi-T5: The T5 model is a natural language processing model developed by Google. Mengzi-T5 is a language model with the same structure as T5. It was pre-trained on a 300G Chinese corpus, capable of being applied to various natural language processing tasks, such as text summarization, machine translation, and question-answering systems.
- ChatGLM: ChatGLM-6B is an open-source, bilingual (Chinese-English) dialogue language model based on the General Language Model (GLM) architecture, with 6.2 billion parameters. With model light-weighting techniques, users can deploy it locally on consumer-grade graphics cards (requiring as low as 6GB of VRAM at the INT4 quantization level).
- GPT-2: As a generative pre-trained model, GPT-2 can generate diverse content based on input text and is widely used in tasks such as dialogue and story generation.

It is observable that the generated outcomes by GPT-2 are exceedingly monotonous; the five generated arguments only differ slightly at the end of the text, with the rest being largely identical while our model can generate logically sound, topically relevant, and diverse arguments.

Arg-T5 was compared with three text generation models under the same conditions. The comparison results are shown in Table 3.

5   Ablation Experiments

To assess the contribution of different factors, we conducted an ablation study presented in Table 4. In this section, we demonstrate the two critical factors in data processing: the addition of perspective classification features and prompt fine-tuning techniques.

Without perspective: In this setup, we do not incorporate perspective classification features into the input text but directly use the original text with prompt words for training. By keeping the amount of training data consistent, we can analyze the impact of perspective features on the quality and coherence of the model-generated text.

Without prompt finetuning: In this setup, we do not fine-tune the model with prompts but directly use the model fine-tuned with data that includes perspective features for text generation. The experiment shows that prompt fine-tuning helps the model understand task instructions and generate text that meets expectations.

Through these ablation experiments, we can gain an in-depth understanding of the contribution of each data processing step to the final text generation effect. We believe that the perspective features enables model to generate arguments from specific viewpoints, thereby improving the diversity of the generated results and addressing the issue of homogenization. The prompt templates help model clearly understand that the task is to generate arguments rather than other types of text, thus enhancing the professionalism of the generated output.

Table 2. After fine-tuning with the training set, the generated arguments of Arg-T5 and the GPT-2 model under the debate topic *Assimilation is More Terrible*.

Model Output	
Arg-T5 (Ours)	Outputs
1. 我方认为被同化的可怕,其实是指当个体失去自我完善的可能。(Our side believes that the horror of assimilation refers to the situation where an individual loses the possibility of self-improvement.) 2. 所以您方的论证不能成立,我方觉得今天被同化的比较标准其实很可悲。(Therefore, your side's argument does not hold up. The standard of comparison for assimilation today is quite lamentable.) 3. 当一个社会或群体的成员逐渐放弃自己的传统和价值观,转而接受主流文化时,他们失去了独特的视角和解决问题的方法。(When members of a society or group gradually abandon their traditions and values in favor of mainstream culture, they lose their unique perspectives and approaches to problem-solving.) 4. 这种文化同化的趋势不仅威胁到了人类文化遗产的保存,也破坏了社会和谐的根基。(This trend of cultural assimilation not only threatens the preservation of human cultural heritage but also undermines the foundation of social harmony.) 5. 文化同化与文化多样性之间的对比揭示了一个关键的现实:同化可能在短期内带来表面的和谐,但从长远来看,却牺牲了文化多样性所提供的创新和适应性。(The comparison between cultural assimilation and cultural diversity reveals a crucial reality: while assimilation may bring about superficial harmony in the short term, it sacrifices the innovation and adaptability that cultural diversity offers in the long run.)	1. 您方今天告诉我说今天我们要讨论的是什么?我方想告诉您一件事情叫什么,叫做你不要伤害别人,你要保护好自己。(What did you tell me we are discussing today? I want to inform you of something: You should not harm others. You must protect yourself.) 2. 您方今天告诉我说今天我们要讨论的是什么?我方想告诉您一件事情叫什么,叫做你不要伤害别人,你要保护好自己,我要告诉你的是你自己。(What did you tell me we are discussing today? I want to inform you of something: You should not harm others. You must protect yourself. What I want to convey to you is about yourself.) 3. 您方今天告诉我说今天我们要讨论的是什么?我方想告诉您一件事情叫什么,叫做你不要伤害别人,你要保护好自己,我们要怎么样去看待一个群体。(What did you tell me we are discussing today? I want to inform you of something: You should not harm others. You must protect yourself. How should we view a group?) 4.您方今天告诉我说今天我们要讨论的是什么?我方想告诉您一件事情叫什么,叫做你不要伤害别人。那好,我们看淡一切事物的本质是在于人性和行为之间的偏差。(What did you tell me we are discussing today? I want to inform you of something: You should not harm others. Well, we perceive that the essence of all things lies in the deviation between human nature and behavior.) 5. 您方今天告诉我说今天我们要讨论的是什么?我方想告诉您一件事情叫什么,叫做你不要伤害别人。那好,我们看淡一切事物的本质是在于人性和价值之间的偏差。(What did you tell me we are discussing today? I want to inform you of something: You should not harm others. Well, we consider the essence of all things to be the discrepancy between human nature and values.)

Table 3. Comparisons of results of different models.

Model	ROUGE-1	ROUGE-2	ROUGE-L
Arg-T5 (ours)	**0.178**	**0.042**	**0.176**
Mengzi-T5	0.122	0.005	0.091
ChatGLM	0.145	0.017	0.139
GPT-2	0.159	0.032	0.155

Table 4. Ablation study. *Perspective* refers to the addition of viewpoint features. *Prompt finetuning* refers to the process of prompt fine-tuning.

Model	ROUGE-1	ROUGE-2	ROUGE-L
Arg-T5 (Ours)	**0.178**	**0.042**	**0.176**
w/o perspective	0.142	0.007	0.103
w/o prompt finetuning	0.155	0.036	0.159
w/o both of the two factors	0.122	0.005	0.091

6 Conclusion

This paper introduces an innovative multi-perspective argument generation method designed to tackle text generation tasks based on debate topics. This approach leverages pre-trained language models and integrates multi-perspective features with prompt fine-tuning techniques to generate high-quality arguments that support debate topics from various perspectives and aspects. We conducted comparative experiments with different generative models, including Mengzi-T5, ChatGLM, and GPT-2, and performed ablation studies to demonstrate the effectiveness of the proposed method. The experimental results indicate that our method significantly improves the Chinese arguments generation task, particularly excelling in maintaining the diversity of generated arguments.

Although this paper has made some progress in multi-perspective argument generation, we must acknowledge that this task still has issues. Future research could attempt to use classification models to automatically categorize each argument before incorporating perspective features into the training part, which may further enhance the model's understanding of perspective features. We could also consider incorporating more features. In addition, the scarcity of debate-related datasets is an issue, collecting more debate-related data and integrating it into a high-quality dataset is another task we wish to achieve in the future. Finally, we hope to investigate an evaluation metric to assess the diversity of the generated arguments. Our model outperformed the models mentioned above on the CCAC2023 dataset, achieving better results.

References

1. O'Neill, J.M., Laycock, C., Scales, R.L.: Argumentation and Debate. Macmillan, London (1927)
2. Van, E.F.H.: Reasonableness and effectiveness in argumentative discourse. Argumentation Libr. **27** (2015)
3. Wei, Z.Y.: 计算论辩技术:迈向智能人类辩手之路, 世界科学 (5),46–49 (2023)
4. Raffel, C., et al.: Exploring the limits of transfer learning with a unified text-to-text transformer. J. Mach. Learn. Res. **21**(140), 1–67 (2020)
5. Zhang, Z.S., et al.: Mengzi: towards lightweight yet ingenious pre-trained models for Chinese. arXiv preprint arXiv:2110.06696 (2021)
6. McKeown, K.: Text Generation. Cambridge University Press, Cambridge (1992)
7. Fine, S., Singer, Y., Tishby, N.: The hierarchical hidden Markov model: analysis and application. Mach. Learn. **32**, 41–62 (1998)
8. Mauldin, M.L.: Semantic rule based text generation. In: Proceedings of the 10th International Conference on Computational Linguistics and 22nd Annual Meeting of the Association for Computational Linguistics, pp. 376–380 (1984)
9. Mikolov, T., Karafiát, M., Burget, L., et al.: Recurrent neural network based language model. In: Interspeech, vol. 2, no. 3, pp. 1045–1048 (2010)
10. Hochreiter, S., Schmidhuber, J.: Long short-term memory. Neural Comput. **9**(8), 1735–1780 (1997)
11. Chung, J.Y., et al.: Empirical evaluation of gated recurrent neural networks on sequence modeling. arXiv preprint arXiv:1412.3555 (2014)
12. Vaswani, A., Shazeer, N., Parmar, N., et al.: Attention is all you need. In: Advances in Neural Information Processing Systems, vol. 30 (2017)
13. Radford, A., Wu, J., Child, R., Luan, D., Amodei, D., Sutskever, I., et al.: Language models are unsupervised multitask learners. OpenAI Blog **1**(8), 9 (2019)
14. Lewis, M., Liu, Y., Goyal, N., et al.: BART: denoising sequence-to-sequence pre-training for natural language generation, translation, and comprehension. In: Proceedings of the 58th Annual Meeting of the Association for Computational Linguistics, pp. 7871–7880 (2020)
15. Freitag, M., Al-Onaizan, Y.: Beam search strategies for neural machine translation. In: Proceedings of the First Workshop on Neural Machine Translation. Association for Computational Linguistics (2017)

MRCJE: A Machine Reading Comprehension Framework with Joint Coding for Emotion-Cause Pair Extraction

Hongsong Wang[✉], Zhide Guo, Ran Tao, Jiale Liu, Yongsheng Luo, Zhiwei Yi, and Yifan Lin

South China Normal University, Guangzhou, China
wanghongsong@m.scnu.edu.cn

Abstract. Emotion-Cause Pair Extraction (ECPE) task, which aims at identifying and extract emotion clauses and corresponding cause clauses. Existing approaches typically employ sequential encoding of features in a predetermined order, which results in imbalanced feature interactions between tasks, whereby information can only flow from the *emotion/cause* clause encoder to the pair encoder. Additionally, the approach is not sensitive to long-distance *emotion-cause pairs*, and the relatively low precision of the extracted ground for cause clauses. To address these issues, this paper proposes a method for Emotion-Cause Pair Extraction based on the **M**achine **R**eading **C**omprehension (MRC) framework with **J**oint **C**oding (MRCJE). This method improves the accuracy of auxiliary tasks such as emotion extraction and cause extraction by concatenating queries and clause displays. It also uses an undirected isomorphic graph to transfer information between clauses and pairs, and generates both pairs and clause features to model causal relationships in clauses, balancing the information flow between emotion clauses, cause clauses and pairs. The method was experimentally demonstrated on a Chinese benchmark corpus, and the results demonstrated that it achieved better results than the baseline model.

Keywords: Emotion-Cause pair extraction · Joint Encoding · Machine reading comprehension

1 Introduction

The Emotion Cause Extraction (ECE) task proposed by Lee et al. [12] aims at extracting causes and certain emotion labels from input documents. However, it relies on prior annotation of emotions in the document, which requires manual input and takes a lot of time. Therefore, Xia and Ding [21] propose a new task called *emotion-cause* pair extraction (ECPE). Given a document as input, ECPE extracts clauses that express emotions and their corresponding clauses that express causes.(As shown in Fig. 1) Intuitively, ECPE is more challenging because the clause classification task and the pair matching task needs to be done simultaneously.

© The Author(s), under exclusive license to Springer Nature Switzerland AG 2025
X. Pan et al. (Eds.): AIMS 2024, LNCS 15421, pp. 63–77, 2025.
https://doi.org/10.1007/978-3-031-77681-6_5

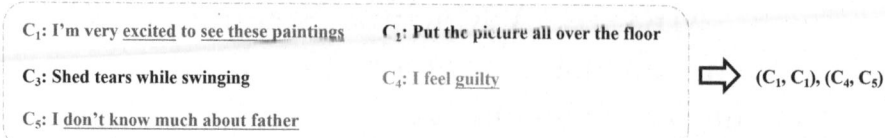

C_1: I'm very <u>excited</u> to <u>see these paintings</u> C_2: Put the picture all over the floor

C_3: Shed tears while swinging C_4: I feel <u>guilty</u>

C_5: I <u>don't know much about father</u>

$(C_1, C_1), (C_4, C_5)$

Fig. 1. An example of the *emotion-cause* pair extraction (ECPE) task. The objective of the ECPE task is to extract the set of *emotion-cause pairs*: $[(c_1, c_1); (c_4, c_5)]$. Underlining highlights the emotion token and the corresponding cause.

Emotion-cause pair extraction poses a distinct set of challenges compared to the task of extracting causes for given emotions. Previous studies in *emotion-cause* pair extraction can be broadly categorized into two approaches: the pipeline model and the end-to-end model. And then Zhou et al. [23] formalised the ECPE task as a document-level MRC task and proposed a multi-round MRC framework with a *rethink* mechanism. Although these methods improve the effectiveness of ECPE's approach, they still have the following limitations. **(1)Errors resulting from an imbalanced flow of information:** Sequential encoding considers only the internal relationships within pairs or clauses, and thus ignores the interrelationships between them. Consequently, if the *emotion/cause* clause encoder makes an erroneous prediction, it will significantly mislead the pair's prediction. An imbalanced flow of information, whereby information flows from clauses to pairs, may result in this error being triggered. *(2)Insensitivity to long-distance emotion-causes:* Most recent models (ECPE-MLL [8] and SLSN [6]) set a fixed-size window around a particular clause and form candidate pairs of central clauses with other clauses within the window. However, models that rely heavily on relative positional features ignore semantic cues over long distances, resulting in position-insensitive data, making the extraction of cause clauses that are distant from the emotion clause poorly generalised. **(3)Inaccuracy in cause clause extraction:** In contrast to the extraction of emotion clauses, the extraction of cause clauses has a lower precision, because the existing methods are not able to take full advantage of their causality during the extraction of emotion clauses and cause clauses, and to validate the results of erroneous extractions. Moreover, it is more difficult to extract cause clauses than emotion clauses explicitly represented by emotion words.

In consideration of the preceding discussion, this paper proposes an emotion cause pair extraction method based on the machine reading comprehension framework with joint coding. The MRC framework is employed to model the relationship between emotion clauses and cause clauses, and the relationship between *emotion/cause* clauses and pairs is modelled through a heterogeneous undirected graph. Thereafter, the emotion clauses and cause clauses are extracted through explicit concatenation. Our experiments conducted on a Chinese benchmark corpus demonstrate that our model significantly outperforms previous benchmarks. This paper summarises the contributions as follows:

1. Information enhancement of clauses using keywords and introduction of an external commonsense knowledge base to obtain finer-grained clause representations.
2. This paper constructs undirected isomorphic graphs to model both *emotion/cause* clauses and the relationships between pairs to learn the causal relationships.
3. This paper validates the effectiveness of *emotion/cause* clause learning by using the MRC framework that includes *rethink*, and using the results of pairs after prediction as queries with the *rethink* mechanism.
4. This paper conducts experiments on the ECPE benchmark corpus and achieves better results than the baseline model.

2   Related Work

2.1   Extraction Cause Pair Extraction

The Emotion Cause Extraction (ECE) task was proposed by Lee et al. [12] as a way to identify the causes of emotion statements; however, this task is subject to limitations due to its definition, which requires manual labelling in advance. In response to this, Xia and Ding et al. [21] developed the Emotion Cause Pair Extraction (ECPE) task, a more generalised approach that does not require the initial labelling of emotion clauses and cause clauses. Recently, a series of research works have employed multi-task learning strategies to model ECPE. Xia and Ding [21] introduced a two-step approach, whereby potential emotion and cause clauses are first extracted through multi-task learning, and then matches and filters the candidate pairs. In addition, the previous work uses the 2D Transformer module as well as two variants to model the relationship between *emotion-cause pairs* [7] or the relationship between two clauses of an *emotion-cause* pair using multilevel attention methods [18]. However, such multi-task learning frameworks [7, 17–19, 21] can lead to the issue of error propagation. To address this problem, the previous work used end-to-end methods [2, 4, 5, 11, 20], which can better handle the logical relationship between clause extraction and pair generation than multitask learning can. And there are other methods used to achieve emotion cause pairs extraction task [3, 8, 9, 22], such as sequence labelling methods [10]. Nevertheless, existing methods either suffer from error propagation or fail to effectively capture or express the causal relationships between emotion clauses and cause clauses. Furthermore, they are considered less effective when they are used to extract cause clauses.

2.2   Joint Encoding

Most of the previous work uses sequential encoding to solve ECPE, including the pipeline and unified framework. Specifically, Xia and Ding [21] proposes ECPE task and two auxiliary tasks (EE and CE). It uses a two-stage method that first extracts the emotion and cause clauses and then matches them as pairs using Cartesian product for prediction. These typical sequential encoding models encode the features in a predefined order, which leads to the imbalance of the inter-task feature interaction. Since the interaction between clauses and pairs is unidirectional, and the features in pairs can not flow to clauses. Liu et al. propose a method for joint encoding of ECPE while modelling pairs and clauses, which addresses the problem of imbalance of feature information between tasks. In this paper, the proposed MRC with Joint Encoding for ECPE utilizes the MRC framework to achieve better results in EE and CE, introducing internal and external knowledge for information enhancement to improve the sensitivity of long text.

3   Methods

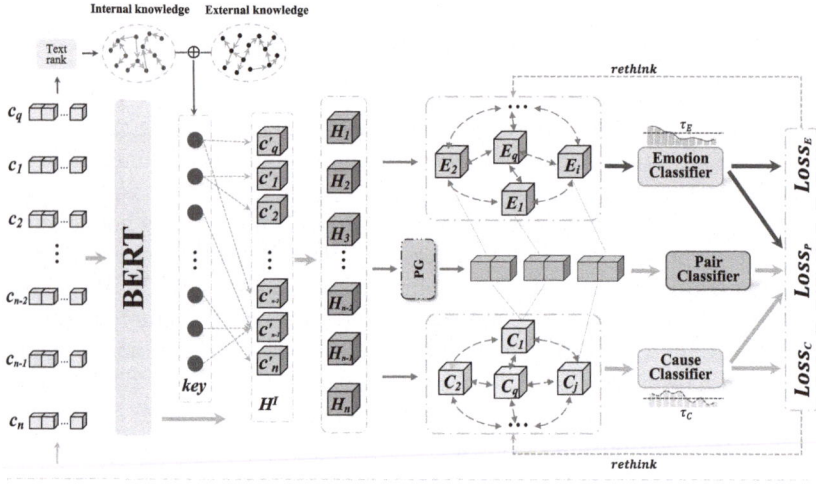

c_1: [CLS]Yesterday afternoon[SEP] c_2: [CLS]I took half an hour trying   [SEP] e_{j1}[CLS] and I ...

Fig. 2. The queries and clauses of emotion and cause clauses are explicitly concatenated, the representation encoded via *BERT* is augmented with information using keywords and externally introduced common-sense knowledge, and then an undirected isomorphic graph is constructed to model the relationship between the *emotion/cause* clauses and the pairs.

3.1   Overview

In this section, we mainly describe our method. Given a document $D = (c_1, c_2, ...c_N)$ consisting of N clauses and each clause contains multiple words $c_i = (w_{i1}, w_{i2}, ..., w_{NM})$, our aim is to extract all the *emotion-causes* pair in D:

$$P = \{..., (c_i, c_j), ...\} (1 \leq i, j \leq N) \tag{1}$$

where the c_i and c_j denote the i-th emotion clause and its corresponding j-th cause clause in D.

3.2   Encoding Layer

This paper utilizes an MRC framework with a *rethink* mechanism in order to extract both emotion clauses and cause clauses. The query is denoted as $q = \{q^e, q^c\}$. $q^e = \{q^{se}, q^{de}\}$, q^{se} is static emotion query: *"Is it an emotion clause?"*, which aims at extracting all the emotion clauses. q^{de} is dynamic emotion query: *"Is it an emotion clause corresponding to c_i?"* which aim to extract the emotion clause corresponding to clause c_i. $q^c = \{q^{sc}, q^{dc}\}$, q^{sc} is static cause query: *"Is it an cause clause?"*, which aims at extracting all the cause clauses. q^{dc} is dynamic cause query: *"Is it a cause clause corresponding to c_i?"* which aim to extract the cause clause corresponding to clause c_i. The query q is then concatenated with the individual clauses. For documents containing N clauses, each containing M words. The input sequence is constructed by inserting a *[CLS]* token at the beginning of each clause and a *[SEP]* token between every two clauses, formally,

$$D^I = \{[CLS], w_{q1}, ..., w_{q|M|}, [SEP], [CLS]w_{11}, w_{12}, ...w_{1|M|}, ..., w_{n|M|}\}, \quad (2)$$

$$H^I = BERT(D^I) = \{c'_{q^e}, c'_{q^c}, c'_1, c'_2, ..., c'_n\}, \quad (3)$$

where $H^I \in \mathbb{R}^{|I| \times d}$ is the embedding of a given document D^I after *BERT*, d is the dimension of the hidden state, c'_n is the hidden representation. Subsequently, each clause representation of H^I is used as a node to construct a clause graph to construct a fully connected clause graph $\mathcal{G} = (v_c, \xi_c)$, where v_c is the set of nodes and ξ_c is the set of edges, and then the attention mechanism is used to model the inter-clause relationships. There exists an edge between every two nodes, and each node has a self-loop edge, node features are initialised by the clause representation c'_n output from *BERT*, and information is propagated between clauses by means of multiple overlapping layers of graph attention, and the representation of nodes v_i^t is denoted as the clause c_i in layer t, formally,

$$v_i^t = ReLU\left(\sum_{j \in N} a_{ij}^t W_1^t v_j^{t-1} + b\right), \quad (4)$$

where N is the neighbouring nodes of node i, $W_1^t \in \mathbb{R}^{d \times d}$ is the learnable transformation matrix, d is the word embedding dimension, b is the bias value, and a_{ij}^t is the attention between neighbouring nodes, formally,

$$a_{ij} = \frac{exp(LeakyReLU(w[W_2^t v_j^{t-1}; W_3^t v_i^{t-1}]))}{\sum_{k \in N} exp(LeakyReLU(w[W_2^t v_k^{t-1}; W_3^t v_i^{t-1}]))}, \quad (5)$$

ultimately, the representation of the individual clauses obtained is

$$H' = \{c'_1, c'_2, ..., c'_n\}. \quad (6)$$

3.3   Information Enhancing

In order to obtain a more fine-grained clause representation, an external knowledge base and keyword information are employed to assist the clause representation in identifying potential causal features. The *TextRank* [16] algorithm is utilized to extract *keywords* from the document, and the *Concept-Net* knowledge base, that is externally introduced, is employed as the emotion lexicon. The concatenation of these two sets constitutes the final keyword set $key = \{k_1, k_2, ..., k_m\}$. Subsequently, the *clause-keyword* bipartite graph $G_k = (v, \xi_k)$ is constructed, where $v = (v'_c \cup v_k)$ represents the set of nodes. The node v'_c is initialised by H', representing the node of a clause, and v_k represents the keyword node, initialised by the word embedding vectors published by Xia and Ding [21]. Finally, the relationship between the clause node v'_c and the keyword node v_k is modelled by the attention mechanism in order to obtain the clause representation H_i, formally,

$$a^k_{ij} = \frac{exp(w[W_4c'_i; W_5k^j])}{\sum_{t \in N} exp(w[W_4c'_t; W_5k_j])},\tag{7}$$

$$e^k_j = \sum_{t \in N} W_6 a^k_{tj} c'_t,\tag{8}$$

$$H_i = tanh((c'_i + \sum_{j \in M} a^k_{ij} e^k_j) + b),\tag{9}$$

where e^k_j is the representation of keyword k_j and b is the bias value. In this way, H_i will have finer-grained characterisation capability.

3.4   Relational Graph Convolutional Networks

Pair Generating. Join representations of two clauses to form a candidate pair.

$$p_{ij} = W_p[h_i; h_j] + b_p + r_{i-j}\tag{10}$$

where $W_p \in \mathbb{R}^{d \times 2d}$ and $b_p \in \mathbb{R}^d$ are learnable parameters, and $r_{i-j} \in R^d$ is the relative position embedding.

Relational Graph Convolutional Networks. This paper uses a relational graph convolutional neural network to capture the interaction information between clauses and between clauses and pairs. This is implemented by constructing an undirected heterogeneous graph $\mathbb{G} = (v, \xi)$, $v = (v^E, v^C, v^P)$ representing the nodes, v^E is the emotion clause node, v^C is the cause clause node, and v^p is the candidate pair node. $\xi = (\xi^{c-c}, \xi^{c-p})$ represents the edges between nodes.

ξ^{c-c}: Represents edges between clause nodes, including *emotion clause-emotion clauses* as well as cause clause-cause clauses, and the corresponding nodes are fully connected to each other to help *emotion/cause* nodes learn contextual information about other *emotion/cause* nodes.

ξ^{c-p}: Indicates edges between clauses and pairs, including *emotion clause-pairs* as well as *cause clause-pairs*, which are the primary means of transmitting information between the clauses that make up a pair, and that are used to convey causality between the two. In addition, each type of node has a self-cycling edge that can help each node maintain its semantic information during interaction. Individual nodes are initialised by the clauses and pairs obtained in the previous section.

$$v_i^E = h_a, \qquad v_j^C = h_b, \qquad v_{p_{ij}}^E = p_{ij}, \tag{11}$$

By means of a graphical convolutional neural network, for the i-th node u in layer t, formally,

$$u_i^t = W_u^t v_u^t + b_u^t \tag{12}$$

$$v_u^{t+1} = ReLU(u_i^t + \sum_{r \in \mathcal{R}} \sum_{l \in \mathcal{N}} \frac{W_r^t v_l^t}{|\mathcal{N}|} + b_r^t) \tag{13}$$

where $\mathcal{R}$ refers to edges of different types, $W_u^t \in \mathbb{R}^{d \times d}$, $b_u^t \in \mathbb{R}$, $W_r^t \in \mathbb{R}^{d \times 2d}$ and $b_r^t \in \mathbb{R}$ are learnable parameters, and $\mathcal{N}$ is the neighbourhood of the node u that is connected to an edge of type r.

Finally, the last layer θ is used as the final representation of all nodes after the convolution operation, formally,

$$E = V_E^\theta, \qquad C = V_C^\theta, \qquad P = V_P^\theta, \tag{14}$$

where E is the final representation of all emotion clauses, C is the final representation of all cause clauses, and P is the final representation of emotion-cause pairs.

Rethink. In order to further filter out the invalid *emotion-cause pairs*, for the emotion clause c_i and cause clause c_j in each pair, after the prediction in the next module, use the dynamic query $q^d = \{q^{de}, q^{dc}\}$ rethink whether it is the corresponding emotion/cause clause as shown in Fig. 2, and finally get the set of valid *emotion-cause pairs*, formally,

$$E_q = c^{ei}, \qquad C_q = c^{cj}, \tag{15}$$

$$p(c^{ei}, c^{cj}) = \lambda p(c^{ei}) p(c^{cj} | c^{ei}), \tag{16}$$

where $c^{ei} \in E$, $c^{cj} \in C$, the weight factor λ is used to adjust the probability of candidate emotion-cause pairs.

3.5   Prediction

After learning the contextual information through graph convolutional neural network, the final clause and pair representations are obtained, after which they are compared with the real labels to calculate their cross entropy and used as a loss function, formally,

$$\mathcal{L}_p = -\sum_i^N \sum_j^N y_{ij}^p \log(\hat{y}_{ij}^p), \mathcal{L}_e = -\sum_i^N y_i^e \log(\hat{y}_i^e), \mathcal{L}_c = -\sum_i^N y_i^c \log(\hat{y}_i^c) \quad (17)$$

where $y_{ij}^p = \sigma(MLP(P, E, C))$. The model is trained by jointly optimising the three subtasks.

$$\mathcal{L} = \alpha \mathcal{L}_p + \beta \mathcal{L}_e + \gamma \mathcal{L}_c \quad (18)$$

where α, β and γ are hype-parameters.

4   Experiments

4.1   Dataset

This paper uses the benchmark dataset released by Xia and Ding [21] for experiments. This typical and widely used dataset is constructed based on an emotion cause extraction corpus that contains 1,945 Chinese documents from SINA city news.

4.2   Baseline Models

- **Indep**: The model independently identifies emotions and causes, then matches emotions with their corresponding causes through a relational mechanism.
- **RANKCP**: A model based on ranking strategies that extracts emotion-cause pairs by leveraging the relative distance embedding of clauses.
- **ECPE-2D**: It uses a two-dimensional matrix to represent emotion-cause pairs and capture interactions between different pairs.
- **PBJE**: It designs a method using joint encoding for extracting emotion-cause pairs by constructing heterogeneous graphs and simultaneously encoding both clauses and clause pairs, ultimately extracting emotion-cause pairs through joint learning of clauses and clause pairs.
- **ECPEE2E**: End-to-end extraction of emotions and causes through multi-task learning, simultaneously recognizing and matching emotion-cause pairs.
- **MGSAG**: It uses a multi-granularity attention mechanism to associate emotions and causes at different levels, enabling emotion-cause pair extraction.
- **KMGP**: It utilizes knowledge graphs and multi-view graph networks to relate emotions and causes, achieving precise extraction of emotion-cause pairs.
- **GAT-ECPE**: It employs graph attention networks to capture dependencies between clauses and jointly extract and match emotion-cause pairs.
- **MM-R**: It utilizes multi-task learning and contrastive positive-negative sampling to jointly extract and optimize the matching of emotion-cause pairs.
- **CFC-ECPE**: It captures contextual associations through cross-clause feature interactions, jointly extracting emotion-cause pairs.

Table 1. The results of MRCJE and the baseline comparison on the Chinese dataset

Approach	Emotion-Cause Pair Extraction			Emotion Clause Extraction			Cause Clause Extraction		
	F1	P	R	F1	P	R	F1	P	R
Indep [21]	68.32	50.82	58.18	83.75	80.71	82.10	69.02	56.73	62.05
Inter-CE [21]	69.02	51.35	59.01	84.94	81.22	83.00	68.09	56.34	61.51
Inter-EC [21]	67.21	57.05	61.28	83.64	81.07	82.30	70.41	60.83	65.07
E2EECPE [17]	64.91	61.95	63.15	85.52	80.24	82.75	70.48	61.59	65.81
RANKCP [20]	73.60	71.19	76.30	90.57	91.23	89.99	76.15	74.61	77.88
ECPE2D [14]	68.89	72.92	65.44	89.10	86.27	92.21	1c71.23	73.36	69.34
PBJE [13]	76.37	79.22	73.84	88.76	90.77	86.91	78.78	81.79	78.78
MGSAG [1]	68.46	72.43	65.07	82.87	87.21	79.11	70.80	75.10	67.13
KMGP [25]	67.32	74.25	62.08	84.79	85.22	84.43	66.42	72.75	61.33
GAT-ECPE [24]	74.92	72.65	77.52	1c90.99	90.98	91.03	78.34	76.17	78.72
MM-R [23]	78.76	80.17	77.40	91.44	94.63	88.46	79.10	80.66	77.60
CFC-ECPE [15]	79.82	**81.41**	78.29	93.10	91.34	**94.92**	81.36	**82.20**	80.54
MRCJE(OURS)	**81.21**	80.03	**82.43**	**94.01**	94.85	93.18	**81.86**	82.13	**81.59**

4.3 Overall Result

As shown in Table 1: Compared to previous emotion cause pair extraction tasks, our modelling approach has significant advantages. On the main task, our model approach improves the F1 value and the recall rate by 1.39% and 4.14% over the most effective baseline model CFC-ECPE compared to previous tasks. And on the emotion extraction task EE task, the F1 values 1.09% over CFC-ECPE and precision rate are improved by 0.22% over MM-R. And on the auxiliary task cause extraction CE, our model made some improvements, with F1 value and recall improved by 0.5% and 1.05% over CFC-ECPE, which is more obvious compared to other baseline models. By analysing the results, this paper believes that the reason why our model can improve over the baseline model for the emotion cause pair extraction task is the enhancement in the performance of the cause extraction task. This is due to the fact that this paper used the framework of MRC and using the results of pairs after prediction as queries with the *rethink* mechanism after the joint coding of the sum clauses.

4.4 Ablation Study

In order to verify the validity of the MRC framework and joint coding, ablation experiments were conducted on both modules and Table 2 shows the results of the Ablation Study.

w/o MRC: In order to verify the effectiveness of MRC in ECPE, this paper will carry out disambiguation experiments on the query $q = \{q^e,\ q^c\}$, as shown in Table 2, in the case of explicitly concatenating the query with the clause in the document is better than that without explicit connection of the model, and compared with the disambiguation experiments of other modules, the use of the MRC has the most obvious effect on the results. This paper analysed the results because explicitly concatenating the query with the clause can be more effective in obtaining information about the *emotion/cause* in the clauses, and *rethink* can also better filter out some negative samples, which in turn improves the accuracy.

w/o RGCN: In order to verify the effect of Joint Coding in ECPE, this paper has done further experiments. Firstly, the ablation experiment, as shown in Table 2, this paper uses sequential coding instead of the RGCN part which has used joint coding. Secondly, the clause representations which use keywords for information enhancement are screened out to the *emotion/cause*

Table 2. Results of an ablation study on a baseline corpus of extracted *emotion-cause pairs* and two subtasks

Approach	ECPE	EE	CE
w/o MRC	78.6	76.1	88.8
w/o RGCN	80.2	77.3	90.5
MRCJE(OURS)	81.21	94.01	81.86

clauses, and then pairwise and joint prediction are carried out, and it can be seen from the results of Table 2, which the results using sequential coding have a decreased compared to the use of Joint coding in the model of this paper.

4.5 Effect of the Rethink Mechanism

In order to verify the effectiveness of the *rethink* mechanism, two model variants are designed for comparison experiments in this paper.

ECPE-MRC is an approach that uses the MRC framework, and in contrast to MRCJE, it removes the *rethink* mechanism.

Table 3. Performance of variants

Approach	ECPE	EE	CE
ECPE-MRC	78.8	93.4	78.1
MRC-SQ	79.2	93.7	70.4
MRCJE(OURS)	81.21	94.01	81.86

MRC-SQ uses the *rethink* mechanism, but in contrast to MRCJE, the query statement it uses in the second round of judgement is the static query $q^s = \{q^{se},\ q^{sc}\}$. The two variants are compared experimentally with MRCJE, and according to Table 3. MRCJE achieved 2.4%, 0.6% and 3.7% on the three tasks compared to ECPE-MRC, which show the effectiveness of *rethink*. While the results of MRC-SQ are improved in the three task pairs compared to ECPE-MRC, but compared to MRCJE task it is reduced in the three tasks by 2%, 0.3% and 3.4% respectively, which prove that the dynamic query has a better effect in the *rethink* mechanism compared to the static query.

4.6 Effect of the External Knowledge

In order to validate the effectiveness of external knowledge and the differences between different emotion knowledge bases, this paper generates internal knowledge using *Textrank (OURS)* and *COMET* to reason about the logical relationships between clauses, respectively. Furthermore, the effectiveness of using *ConceptNet* as external knowledge is also validated (Table 4).

The experimental results demonstrate that the utilisation of COMET for the extraction of keywords for inter-sentence logical analysis has the effect on reducing the ECPE by 5.08%, while the two auxiliary tasks of EE and CE are reduced by 4.08% and 5.40%, respectively. These findings indicate that COMET is a more effective approach than Textrank for the extraction of key information between clauses and cause about logical relationships. In the

Table 4. Results of validating the effectiveness of the External Knowledge

Approach	ECPE	EE	CE
w COMET	76.13	89.93	76.46
w/o ConceptNet	76.52	90.22	77.91
MRCJE(OURS)	81.21	94.01	81.86

context of keyword extraction, TextRank demonstrates superior accuracy compared to COMET. This is attributed to TextRank's capacity to establish logical relationships that align more closely with common sense, through the evaluation of sentence-to-sentence relationships through a similarity-based graph model. Conversely, the use of COMET for the analysis of logical relationships between clauses, in conjunction with the introduction of an external knowledge base (ConceptNet), resulted in a decrease of 4.69%, 3.79% and 3.95% in ECPE, EE and CE, respectively. This demonstrates the efficacy of COMET in analysing the logical relationships between clauses, particularly when coupled with an external knowledge.

4.7   Study of the Distance Between Emotions and Causes

To evaluate the performance of MRCJE in extracting *emotion-cause pairs* between different distances, this paper uses MRCJE and two benchmark models RankCP and PBJE for pairs (c_i, c_j) of two cases in the dataset, with a relative position of 1 or less ($|i - j| \leq 1$) and with a relative position greater than or equal to 2 ($|i - j| \geq 2$), respec-

Table 5. The results of ECPE for pairs of different relative positions.

Relative Position	Approach	P	R	F
	RankCP	77.45	83.38	80.31
	PBJE	80.69	81.26	80.97
	MRCJE(OURS)	82.71	84.22	83.46
	RankCP	31.60	32.91	32.24
	PBJE	58.55	28.43	38.27
	MRCJE(OURS)	62.97	36.31	46.06

tively, and the experimental results are shown in Table 5. MRCJE outperforms both PBJE and RankCP in cases where the relative position of the *emotion-cause pairs* is less than or equal to 1 and greater than or equal to 2, suggesting that MRCJE can deal with more complex cases. However, since more than 85% of the *emotion-cause pairs* in the dataset have a relative position of 1 or less, and as long as 15% are greater than or equal to 2, the training results in cases where the relative position is greater than or equal to 2 are relatively poor.

4.8   Case Study

This paper has chosen an example from the dataset to demonstrate the effectiveness of the method in this paper, as shown in Table 6, in which c_{12} is the emotion clause, and c_9, c_{10}, and c_{11} are the cause clauses of c_{12}. According to the extraction results of MRCJE and RankCP, c_{12} is predicted to be an affective clause due to the presence of the word "helpless" in c_{12}. However, RankCP extract the wrong clause c_{11} in EE. As can be seen from Fig. 3, both MRCJE and RankCP predict above threshold confidence levels for c_9, c_{10}, c_{11} and c_{12}, so c_9, c_{10}, c_{11} are judged as the cause clauses of c_{12}. Nevertheless, RankCP also extracts erroneous emotion-cause pair $[c_{11}, c_{10}]$. So the *emotion-cause pairs* predicted by MRCJE are $[c_{12}, c_{11}]$, $[c_{12}, c_{10}]$, $[c_{12}, c_9]$, and the *emotion-cause pairs* predicted by RankCP are $[c_{12}, c_{11}]$, $[c_{12}, c_{10}]$, $[c_{12}, c_9]$, $[c_{11}, c_{10}]$. According to Ground Truth it is known that MRCJE accomplishes the correct prediction. And we can find that RankCP tends to extract as many candidate pairs as possible. But there could be many wrong pairs.

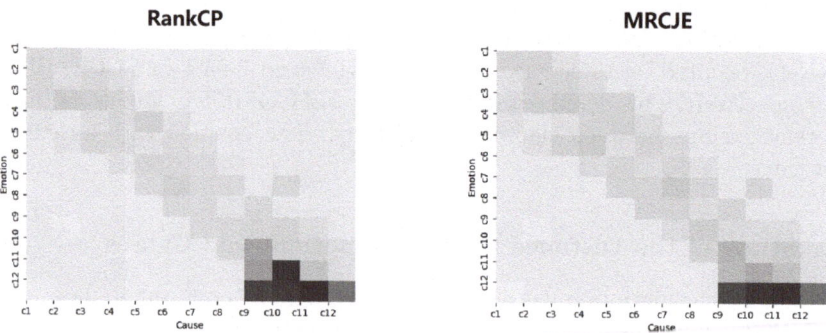

Fig. 3. Visualization of the confidence of each prediction in MRCJE and RankCP. The deeper color means the higher confidence.

Table 6. An example predicted by MRCJE. The words in red denote emotion token, and blue denotes correct prediction results.

(c_1) In order to save the woman as soon as possible, (c_2) commanders immediately developed a rescue plan,âĂ¢âĂ¢, (c_9)she is due to the fact that the other party owes money for the work, (c_{10})and her family was in dire need of money, (c_{11})her life is stressful,(c_{12})she was so hopeless that she chose to jump to her death.	
MRCJE	$[c_{12}, c_{11}], [c_{12}, c_{10}], [c_{12}, c_9]$
RankCP	$[c_{12}, c_{11}], [c_{12}, c_{10}], [c_{12}, c_9], [c_{11}, c_{10}]$
Ground Truth	$[c_{12}, c_{11}], [c_{12}, c_{10}], [c_{12}, c_9]$

5   Conclusion and Future Work

In this paper, a MRC framework with joint encoding ECPE method is proposed, compared with previous models, the causal relationships between emotion clauses and cause clauses can be better modelled by using joint encoding than sequential encoding, using the MRC framework and using the *rethink* mechanism, which links the query and clause displays to improve the *emotion/cause* clause. After modelling the relationship between emotion clauses and cause clauses through heterogeneous graphs, the validity of candidate pairs is verified using the original dynamic query. Experiments on a Chinese benchmark corpus show that the model outperforms previous benchmark models. However, this method still has some limitations, and our experiments were conducted on the Chinese dataset, so the effectiveness of the method in different language environments needs to be experimentally verified. In our future work, we plan to improve our experiments on a multimodal dataset and develop a multimodal emotional cause pair extraction method.

References

1. Bao, Y., Ma, Q., Wei, L., Zhou, W., Hu, S.: Multi-granularity semantic aware graph model for reducing position bias in emotion cause pair extraction. In: Findings of the Association for Computational Linguistics: ACL 2022, pp. 1203–1213 (2022)
2. Cao, W., et al.: Causal narrative comprehension: a new perspective for emotion cause extraction. IEEE Trans. Affect. Comput. **13**(4), 1743–1758 (2022)
3. Chen, S., et al.: Joint alignment of multi-task feature and label spaces for emotion cause pair extraction. In: Proceedings of the 29th International Conference on Computational Linguistics, pp. 6955–6965 (2022)
4. Chen, Y., Hou, W., Li, S., Wu, C., Zhang, X.: End-to-end emotion-cause pair extraction with graph convolutional network. In: Proceedings of the 28th International Conference on Computational Linguistics, pp. 198–207 (2020)
5. Cheng, Z., Jiang, Z., Yin, Y., Wang, C., Ge, S., Gu, Q.: A consistent dual-MRC framework for emotion-cause pair extraction. ACM Trans. Info. Syst. **41**(4), 1–27 (2023)
6. Cheng, Z., Jiang, Z., Yin, Y., Yu, H., Gu, Q.: A symmetric local search network for emotion-cause pair extraction. In: Proceedings of the 28th International Conference on Computational Linguistics, pp. 139–149 (2020)
7. Ding, Z., Xia, R., Yu, J.: Ecpe-2d: Emotion-cause pair extraction based on joint two-dimensional representation, interaction and prediction. In: Proceedings of the 58th Annual Meeting of the Association for Computational Linguistics, pp. 3161–3170 (2020)
8. Ding, Z., Xia, R., Yu, J.: End-to-end emotion-cause pair extraction based on sliding window multi-label learning. In: Proceedings of the 2020 conference on empirical methods in natural language processing (EMNLP), pp. 3574–3583 (2020)
9. Fan, C., Yuan, C., Du, J., Gui, L., Yang, M., Xu, R.: Transition-based directed graph construction for emotion-cause pair extraction. In: Proceedings of the 58th Annual Meeting of the Association for Computational Linguistics, pp. 3707–3717 (2020)

10. Fan, C., Yuan, C., Gui, L., Zhang, Y., Xu, R.: Multi-task sequence tagging for emotion cause pair extraction via tag distribution refinement. IEEE/ACM Trans. Audio Speech Lang. Proces. **29**, 2339–2350 (2021)
11. Fan, R., Wang, Y., He, T.: An end-to-end multi-task learning network with scope controller for emotion-cause pair extraction. In: Zhu, X., Zhang, M., Hong, Yu., He, R. (eds.) NLPCC 2020. LNCS (LNAI), vol. 12430, pp. 764–776. Springer, Cham (2020). https://doi.org/10.1007/978-3-030-60450-9_60
12. Lee, S.Y.M., Chen, Y., Huang, C.R.: A text-driven rule-based system for emotion cause detection. In: Proceedings of the NAACL HLT 2010 Workshop on Computational Approaches to Analysis and Generation of Emotion in Text, pp. 45–53 (2010)
13. Liu, J., Shang, X., Ma, Q.: Pair-based joint encoding with relational graph convolutional networks for emotion-cause pair extraction. In: Proceedings of the 2022 Conference on Empirical Methods in Natural Language Processing, pp. 5339–5351 (2022)
14. Ma, B., et al.: Distant supervision based machine reading comprehension for extractive summarization in customer service. In: Proceedings of the 44th International ACM SIGIR Conference on Research and Development in Information Retrieval, pp. 1895–1899 (2021)
15. Mai, H., Zhang, X., Wang, J., Zhou, X.: A machine reading comprehension model with counterfactual contrastive learning for emotion-cause pair extraction. Knowledge and Information Systems, pp. 1–18 (2024)
16. Mihalcea, R., Tarau, P.: Textrank: bringing order into text. In: Proceedings of the 2004 Conference on Empirical Methods in Natural Language Processing, pp. 404–411 (2004)
17. Song, H., Zhang, C., Li, Q., Song, D.: End-to-end emotion-cause pair extraction via learning to link. arXiv:abs/2002.10710 (2020)
18. Tang, H., Ji, D., Zhou, Q.: Joint multi-level attentional model for emotion detection and emotion-cause pair extraction. Neurocomputing **409**, 329–340 (2020)
19. Vaswani, A., et al.: Attention is all you need. In: Proceedings of the 31st International Conference on Neural Information Processing Systems, pp. 6000–6010 (2017)
20. Wei, P., Zhao, J., Mao, W.: Effective inter-clause modeling for end-to-end emotion-cause pair extraction. In: Proceedings of the 58th Annual Meeting of the Association for Computational Linguistics, pp. 3171–3181 (2020)
21. Xia, R., Ding, Z.: Emotion-cause pair extraction: a new task to emotion analysis in texts. In: Proceedings of the 57th Annual Meeting of the Association for Computational Linguistics. Association for Computational Linguistics (2019)
22. Yang, C., Ding, J.: Emotion-cause pair extraction via transformer-based interaction model with text capsule network. In: Lu, W., Huang, S., Hong, Y., Zhou, X. (eds.) NLPCC 2022. LNCS, vol. 13551, pp. 781–793. Springer, Cham (2022). https://doi.org/10.1007/978-3-031-17120-8_60
23. Zhou, C., Song, D., Xu, J., Wu, Z.: A multi-turn machine reading comprehension framework with rethink mechanism for emotion-cause pair extraction. In: Proceedings of the 29th International Conference on Computational Linguistics, pp. 6726–6735 (2022)

24. Zhu, P., Wang, B., Tang, K., Zhang, H., Cui, X., Wang, Z.: A knowledge-guided graph attention network for emotion-cause pair extraction. Knowl.-Based Syst. **286**, 111342 (2024)

25. Zong, L., Zhang, J., Zhou, J., Zhang, X., Xu, B.: Emotion-cause pair extraction via knowledge-driven multi-classification and graph-based position embedding. Appl. Intell. pp. 1–13 (2024)

AI Value Protocol: Utilizing Blockchain to Promote AI AIVP

Adel ELMessiry[2]([✉]) [iD] and Magdi El Messiry[1,2] [iD]

[1] WebDBTech, Nashville, USA
[2] Alexandria University, Alexandria, Egypt
Adel.ElMessiry@gmail.com

Abstract. The rapid proliferation of artificial intelligence (AI) technologies has introduced unprecedented opportunities across various industries, from healthcare and finance to manufacturing and entertainment. However, the sheer volume of AI projects has created significant challenges in distinguishing meaningful initiatives from those that merely add to the noise. To address this, there is a pressing need for a structured approach to evaluate and promote AI projects that deliver genuine value. The AI Value Protocol (AIVP) presents a comprehensive framework designed to achieve this goal by leveraging blockchain technology to create an immutable record of AI development, ensuring transparency, accountability, and trust throughout the process.

The AIVP framework is built around four critical steps. The first step, AI Discovery, involves identifying and categorizing AI initiatives with the potential for significant positive impact. Blockchain technology is employed to securely record the details and assessments of these projects, providing a transparent and tamper-proof history of their development. The second step, AI Verification, focuses on ensuring the reliability, accuracy, and ethical standards of AI systems through rigorous testing and validation. Blockchain is again utilized to log verification processes and outcomes, creating an immutable record that stakeholders can trust, free from tampering or bias.

Following verification, AI Certification is granted to projects that meet established benchmarks for quality, ethics, and performance, with certification data stored on the blockchain to offer a verifiable and permanent record of credibility. Finally, AI Incentivization encourages the development and deployment of high-value AI projects by creating incentives for innovation, ethical practices, and long-term sustainability. Blockchain facilitates the tracking and rewarding of contributions, ensuring that incentives are distributed fairly and transparently.

For instance, in healthcare, AI projects focused on predictive diagnostics or AI-enhanced medical imaging can benefit from AIVP by ensuring transparency in their decision-making algorithms, providing robust verification for ethical standards, and incentivizing real-world impact. Similarly, in finance, AI systems offering fraud detection or market forecasting could gain credibility through verified blockchain records, increasing stakeholder trust. These use cases emphasize AIVP's relevance in diverse industries.

© The Author(s), under exclusive license to Springer Nature Switzerland AG 2025
X. Pan et al. (Eds.): AIMS 2024, LNCS 15421, pp. 78–90, 2025.
https://doi.org/10.1007/978-3-031-77681-6_6

Through the integration of blockchain technology, the AI Value Protocol offers a robust mechanism for filtering through the vast array of AI developments, highlighting those that truly contribute to societal progress. By providing an immutable and secure record of the entire process, AIVP fosters greater trust among stakeholders and empowers organizations, policymakers, and developers to navigate the AI landscape responsibly and effectively.

Keywords: AI · Artificial Intelligence · Blockchain

1   Introduction

In recent years, the rapid proliferation of artificial intelligence (AI) technologies has ushered in a new era of innovation and possibilities across various industries [9]. However, this meteoric rise in AI adoption has brought to the forefront several critical challenges that the Artificial Intelligence Value Protocol (AIVP) aims to address [19].

1.1   Lack of Value Verification

The AI landscape is flooded with a myriad of solutions, but assessing their actual value and impact remains a daunting task. There is a pressing need for a standardized framework to verify and quantify the value created by AI projects. Without such verification, stakeholders are left in the dark about the true benefits of these technologies. A case in point is the collapse of the AI startup **Theranos**, which misrepresented its technological capabilities to investors, leading to massive losses and undermining trust across the industry [6].

1.2   Ethical Concerns

The opacity of AI algorithms and decision-making processes raises ethical concerns, particularly regarding issues of bias, fairness, and accountability. Without transparency and accountability mechanisms, AI systems can perpetuate discriminatory practices, eroding trust in the technology [4,7]. For example, facial recognition algorithms have been shown to exhibit racial bias in law enforcement, leading to wrongful arrests and broader civil rights violations [2].

1.3   Fraudulent Practices

The absence of a robust certification system has paved the way for fraudulent claims in the AI domain. Some AI projects overstate their capabilities and impact, misleading investors, users, and stakeholders. This not only undermines trust but also hinders the growth of genuine AI innovations. In addition to Theranos, there are multiple cases where AI systems misrepresent their efficacy in sectors like healthcare, where unverified diagnostic tools have led to dangerous misdiagnoses [16].

1.4   Incentivization Gap

AI developers often lack proper incentives to prioritize value creation over profit maximization. As a result, there is a disconnect between technological advancement and genuine societal benefit. An effective incentivization mechanism is needed to align the interests of AI developers with the broader community.

1.5   Fragmented Ecosystem

The current AI ecosystem lacks a unified platform for users to discover, assess, and engage with value-driven AI projects. This fragmentation inhibits collaboration and makes it difficult for users to make informed decisions about which AI solutions to adopt.

1.6   Opaque Financial Reporting

Determining the actual financial value generated by AI projects remains a significant challenge. This opaqueness hampers investment decisions and limits the ability to track the real impact of AI on various industries.

The AIVP recognizes these pressing challenges as barriers to the responsible and sustainable advancement of AI. By providing a standardized framework for value verification, ethical considerations, certification, and incentivization, the AIVP seeks to bridge the gap between AI innovation and genuine societal benefit, fostering a transparent and accountable AI ecosystem for all stakeholders.

2   Why Use Blockchain Technology?

Blockchain technology offers numerous advantages in the context of the Artificial Intelligence Value Protocol (AIVP) [13]. These advantages not only enhance the protocol's core functionalities but also address some of the critical challenges in the AI landscape. Here are the key advantages of using blockchain in the AIVP:

2.1   Transparency and Immutability

Blockchain is inherently transparent, as it records all transactions and interactions in a decentralized ledger [8]. This transparency ensures that all stakeholders in the AIVP ecosystem can verify and trace activities, making it difficult for any party to manipulate or falsify data. Immutability ensures that once data is recorded, it cannot be altered, enhancing trust and accountability [10].

2.2   Security

Blockchain employs advanced cryptographic techniques to secure data and transactions. In the AIVP, this means that user identities, project certifications, and financial transactions are protected against unauthorized access, fraud, and cyberattacks. Users can trust that their information is secure within the protocol [15].

2.3   Decentralization

The decentralized nature of blockchain eliminates the need for intermediaries. In the AIVP, this reduces reliance on centralized authorities for certification and verification, fostering a more inclusive and collaborative environment. It also reduces the risk of a single point of failure, enhancing system resilience [5].

2.4   Smart Contracts

Smart contracts are self-executing agreements with predefined rules and conditions. They automate processes in the AIVP, such as certification, financial transactions, and rewards distribution, reducing the need for manual intervention and potential errors. Smart contracts ensure that all parties in the ecosystem are held accountable to agreed-upon terms [11].

2.5   Trust and Accountability

Blockchain's transparency, security, and immutability create a high level of trust within the AIVP ecosystem. AI developers, users, and auditors can rely on the veracity of data and certifications recorded on the blockchain, fostering trust and accountability in the value verification process [14].

2.6   Incentivization Mechanism

The AIVP token, powered by blockchain, serves as the protocol's medium of exchange and incentivization rewards. Its utilization is transparent and auditable, ensuring that AI projects receive fair compensation for their contributions. Blockchain also enables the purchase of AIVP tokens from the open market, which can stimulate demand and value appreciation.

2.7   Data Integrity

In the AIVP, data integrity is crucial for recording AI-generated value accurately. Blockchain's immutability guarantees that once a value is recorded, it remains unchanged. This is particularly important in financial certifications, where the accuracy of value generated is paramount [1].

2.8   Interoperability

Blockchain technology can be compatible with various blockchain networks and protocols. This interoperability potential allows the AIVP to integrate seamlessly with other blockchain-based solutions, expanding its reach and utility within the broader AI ecosystem [3].

2.9   User Empowerment

Blockchain technology empowers users by giving them greater control over their data and assets. In the AIVP, this means that users have more agency in managing their identities, engaging with AI projects, and participating in the protocol's governance.

In summary, blockchain technology provides a solid foundation for the AIVP, addressing many of the challenges and needs in the AI landscape. Its transparency, security, automation, and trust-enhancing features make it an ideal choice for verifying and incentivizing value-driven AI projects while fostering a more transparent, accountable, and collaborative ecosystem.

3   AIVP Overview

AIVP aims to promote and incentivize value-driven AI projects using blockchain. The protocol will become the premiere destination to discover, engage, and evolve verified value-driven AI projects. The ecosystem will allow AI users and AI developers to interact with each other in a secure and verified environment. The entire ecosystem is powered by the AIVP token which serves as [12] (Fig. 1):

- The medium of exchange
- The incentivization rewards
- The governance mechanism

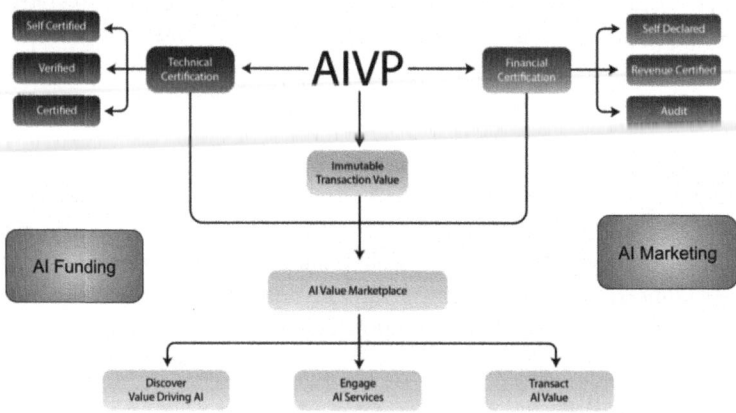

Fig. 1. AIVP Overview

3.1   Technical Certification

The technology certification focuses on the project's technology delivery. It answers the question: "Do the project APIs produce the claimed results?" To illustrate, an AI project that claims to detect fraud in real-time would need to provide its algorithms for rigorous verification before receiving certification. This transparency helps ensure that only legitimate AI projects receive AIVP certification, maintaining trust in the ecosystem.

Self-certification. Any project can self-register and provide attestation to what they can achieve. By self-certification, the project will be assigned a blockchain-unique address and identity. This entry-level certification is similar to how certain ISO certifications allow companies to self-declare conformity with minimal oversight.

Verified. A project can request the AIP team to verify the generated value. The request will be sent to the AIVP verifiers available. A minimum of three certified AIVP verifiers are required to reach a consensus on the verification. Verified certification could also be compared to established models like **SOC 2 Type 2** certifications, where verifiers must audit and confirm the compliance of a system with specific standards.

Certified. When a project requests the AIVP certification, the project will provide full access to the algorithms so that the AIVP verifiers can study the actual algorithm and certify its validity. This level of transparency surpasses many traditional certification frameworks, ensuring deeper accountability and trust.

3.2   AIVP Financial Certification

Financial certification focuses on recording the actual value produced by the project. The financial certification has three levels namely, self-certified, revenue certified, and audited.

Financial Self-certification. Any project that participates in the protocol can report its AI-generated value by calling the API or directly calling the smart contract with the generated value parameters and 5% of the generated value. The smart contract will record the value and return 4.5% back to the project in the form of AIVP token equivalent

Revenue Certification. In the revenue certification level, the projects send the entire revenue of each delivered. AI value to the protocol. This way, the full value is tracked on the blockchain, and the protocol will automatically deduct 5% from the value and send the remaining 95% to the designated project wallet address. The protocol will also send 4.5% back to the project wallet in the form of the AIVP token as is the case with the self-certification.

Full Audit Certification. In the full audit certification, the actual account payables are certified through a third-party accounting firm, which will review the actual payables of the project and issue a Certificate for them before sending 95% of the revenue back to the project wallet. Just like with the revenue certification, the protocol will also automatically send 4.5% of the value back to the appropriate wallet in the form of the AI VP token.

4   Token Economics

AI projects receive **AIVP** tokens as rewards from the grants pool based on their level of participation and the value they deliver. These tokens are given as an incentive for projects to adhere to the protocol's standards and contribute transparently.

Token rewards are distributed based on the certification level achieved by projects, with higher certification levels receiving greater rewards.

AIVP charges a nominal fee of 0.5% for various transactions within the ecosystem, such as certification requests and financial reporting. This fee is typically a small percentage of the transaction value and is collected in **AIVP** tokens [18] (Fig. 2).

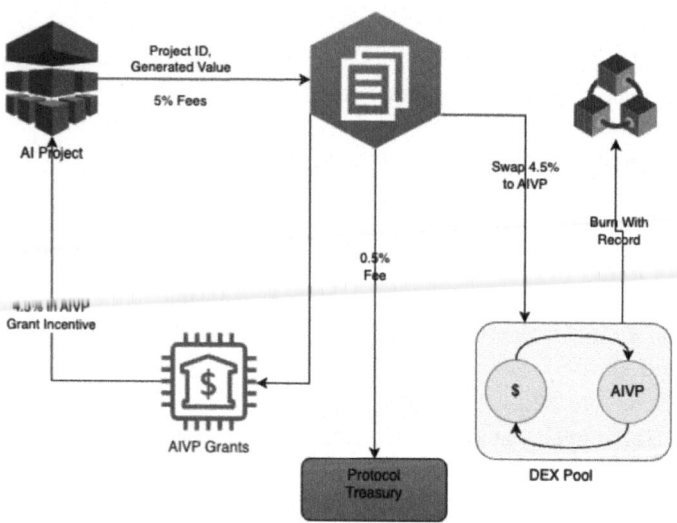

Fig. 2. Token Economics

5   Proof of Stake Verifiers (PoSV) in AIVP

The Proof of Stake Verifiers (PoSV) system is a crucial component of the AI Value Protocol (AIVP), designed to ensure the integrity and reliability of the verification process while aligning the incentives of verifiers with the overall success of the network.

5.1 Staking Requirement

Participation in Verification Pool: To become a verifier in the AIVP ecosystem, participants must stake a specific amount of AIVP tokens. This staking requirement acts as a security deposit, ensuring that only serious and committed verifiers participate in the process. The staked tokens serve as collateral, which can be slashed in the event of dishonest or incorrect behavior, thus aligning the verifier's incentives with the accuracy and honesty of their work.

5.2 Verification Request (VR) Process

- Odd Number of Verifiers: When a Verification Request (VR) is initiated, it is sent to the verification pool, where it is only accepted if an odd number of verifiers agree to take on the task. This odd number requirement helps prevent ties in voting, ensuring that a clear consensus can be reached.
- Publication of Results and Voting: Each verifier is required to independently assess the VR and publish their verification results alongside their vote. This transparency allows for the comparison of different verifiers' assessments and contributes to the overall trustworthiness of the process.

5.3 Consensus and Rewards

- Reaching Consensus: Once the verifiers have published their results and votes, the system checks for consensus. If a majority agrees, the consensus is recorded, and the VR is considered successfully verified [17].
- Distribution of Rewards: The rewards for successful verification are distributed among the verifiers who participated in the consensus. This reward is paid out in AIVP tokens, providing a financial incentive for accurate and honest verification.

5.4 Slashing Mechanism

Penalty for Failed Verifiers: Verifiers who fail to align with the consensus or are found to have provided incorrect verification results face penalties in the form of slashing their staked tokens. The slashing starts at 10% for the first failure and increases exponentially with subsequent failures. This slashing mechanism discourages dishonest behavior and ensures that only verifiers who are confident in their assessments participate.

5.5   Arbitration Process

- Requesting Arbitration: If a verifier believes that the consensus reached was incorrect, they have the option to request arbitration. To do so, they must initiate a vote and stake double the amount of their original stake. This higher stake reflects the increased risk and responsibility associated with challenging the initial consensus.
- New Set of Verifiers: The arbitration request (AR) triggers a new verification process with a different set of verifiers. These new verifiers re-evaluate the VR to determine if the initial consensus was indeed correct or if an error was made.
- Arbitration Outcomes: If the arbitration is successful, meaning the original consensus is overturned, the verifier who initiated the AR receives all the rewards from the verification process. In contrast, the verifiers who were part of the original, incorrect consensus will have their stakes slashed. If the AR fails, meaning the original consensus is upheld, the verifier who initiated the AR faces the maximum penalty, with their entire stake being slashed.

The PoSV mechanism within AIVP is carefully designed to ensure the integrity of the verification process, align verifier incentives with accuracy and honesty, and provide a clear pathway for resolving disputes. This system enhances the overall reliability and security of the AI Value Protocol, making it a robust platform for AI verification and certification.

6   Conclusion

The AI Value Protocol (AIVP) represents a groundbreaking approach to ensuring the integrity, reliability, and incentivization of AI verification and certification processes. By leveraging the decentralized power of blockchain technology, AIVP offers a transparent, secure, and robust framework that aligns the interests of all participants-users, verifiers, and stakeholders alike.

Key features such as the Proof of Stake Verifiers (PoSV) system, Horus Wallet integration for seamless user authentication, and the use of advanced consensus mechanisms on fast blockchains like Base and Polygon, all contribute to AIVP's resilience and effectiveness. The protocol's commitment to privacy, security, and fault tolerance further underscores its capacity to operate reliably under a wide range of conditions.

AIVP's innovative governance and arbitration processes ensure that the network remains fair and just, providing clear pathways for dispute resolution and maintaining the finality and immutability of records. These measures, combined with a strong focus on interoperability, performance, and resource sustainability, position AIVP as a leading solution in the emerging field of AI value verification.

In conclusion, AIVP not only addresses the current challenges in AI verification but also sets a new standard for how AI systems can be evaluated, certified, and incentivized in a decentralized and trustless environment. Through its carefully designed protocols and strategic use of blockchain technology, AIVP is poised to become a cornerstone in the future of AI governance, offering unparalleled reliability and security in the certification of AI systems.

Acknowledgment. The authors would like to acknowledge AlphaFin, WebDBTech, Health Reasoning, AI Innovation Association, Ahmed Akram, and Open AI for their support.

Appendix

A   Key Terminology

In order to facilitate a clearer understanding of the concepts discussed in this paper, the following definitions provide explanations of the blockchain-specific terms used within the AI Value Protocol (AIVP).

A.1   Blockchain

A decentralized, distributed ledger that records transactions across multiple computers. Blockchain technology ensures that records are secure, immutable, and verifiable without relying on a centralized authority. In the context of AIVP, blockchain is used to securely record the verification and certification of AI projects.

A.2   Immutability

Once data is recorded on the blockchain, it cannot be altered or deleted. This feature ensures that records, such as AI project certifications, remain permanent and tamper-proof. Immutability enhances trust, as stakeholders know the data has not been changed.

A.3   Decentralization

The process of distributing data and control across a network rather than relying on a single central authority. In AIVP, decentralization means that no single entity has control over the verification or certification process, reducing the risk of bias or manipulation.

A.4   Smart Contracts

Self-executing contracts with the terms of the agreement written directly into code. In AIVP, smart contracts automate certification processes and token rewards, ensuring that actions occur automatically when predefined conditions are met. This removes the need for intermediaries and reduces errors.

A.5   Proof of Stake (PoS)

A consensus mechanism used in blockchain where validators (or verifiers) are selected to confirm transactions or data based on the number of tokens they hold and are willing to "stake." In AIVP, PoS ensures that only serious participants with a financial commitment are involved in the verification of AI projects.

A.6   Slashing

A penalty mechanism used in Proof of Stake systems where a portion of the staked tokens is forfeited by a verifier if they act dishonestly or fail to perform their duties accurately. In AIVP, slashing discourages verifiers from making inaccurate or biased assessments during the AI project certification process.

A.7   Consensus

The agreement among participants in a decentralized network about the validity of data or transactions. In the AIVP, a consensus is required among verifiers to certify an AI project. Consensus is necessary to ensure that the verification process is unbiased and trustworthy.

A.8   Arbitration

A process in which disputes over verification results are resolved. In AIVP, verifiers can request arbitration if they believe the consensus reached is incorrect. A new set of verifiers re-evaluates the data to determine the final outcome. This mechanism ensures fairness and accuracy in the certification process.

A.9   Staking

The act of locking up tokens as collateral to participate in blockchain activities, such as verification. In the AIVP, verifiers must stake AIVP tokens to take part in the certification process. If they behave dishonestly or fail, their staked tokens may be partially or fully forfeited (slashed).

A.10   Token Economics

The economic model governing the creation, distribution, and use of tokens within a blockchain ecosystem. In AIVP, tokens are used as a medium of exchange, for governance, and as rewards for participants who contribute to the verification and certification processes.

References

1. Bridgesmith, L., ELMessiry, A., Marei, M.: Legal service delivery and support for the dao ecosystem. In: Chen, S., Shyamasundar, R.K., Zhang, L.J. (eds.) Blockchain - ICBC 2022, pp. 18–28. Springer, Cham (2022)

2. Buolamwini, J., Gebru, T.: Gender shades: intersectional accuracy disparities in commercial gender classification. In: Proceedings of Machine Learning Research, vol. 81, pp. 77–91 (2018)

3. Castro, M., Liskov, B.: Practical byzantine fault tolerance and proactive recovery. ACM Trans. Comput. Syst. (TOCS) **20**(4), 398–461 (2002)

4. Coeckelbergh, M.: AI ethics. Mit Press (2020)

5. Donmez, A., Karaivanov, A.: Transaction fee economics in the ethereum blockchain. Econ. Inq. **60**(1), 265–292 (2022)

6. Elhadidi, M.A.: The impact of ethical failures in ai: a case study of theranos. J. AI Ethics **4**(2), 123–135 (2021)

7. Elmessiry, A., Elmessiry, M., Elmessiry, K.: Unethical use of artificial intelligence in education. In: EDULEARN23 Proceedings, pp. 6703–6707. 15th International Conference on Education and New Learning Technologies, IATED (3-5 July, 2023 2023). https://doi.org/10.21125/edulearn.2023.1764. https://DOI.org/10.21125/edulearn.2023.1764

8. Elmessiry, A., Elmessiry, M., Elmessiry, M., Elmessiry, K.: Bai: A blockchain and artificial intelligence educational planner. In: INTED2023 Proceedings. pp. 5899–5903. 17th International Technology, Education and Development Conference, IATED (6-8 March, 2023 2023). https://doi.org/10.21125/inted.2023.1551. https://DOI.org/10.21125/inted.2023.1551

9. ElMessiry, A., ElMessiry, M., Spiceland, D.: Leveraging the artificial intelligence value protocol (aivp) for educational enhancement. In: EDULEARN24 Proceedings, pp. 7099–7103. 16th International Conference on Education and New Learning Technologies, IATED (1-3 July, 2024 2024). https://doi.org/10.21125/edulearn.2024.1679. https://DOI.org/10.21125/edulearn.2024.1679

10. ElMessiry, M., ElMessiry, A.: Blockchain framework for textile supply chain management. In: International Conference on Blockchain, pp. 213–227. Springer (2018)

11. Elmessiry, M., Elmessiry, A.: Crypto copycat: a fashion centric blockchain framework for eliminating fashion infringement. Int. J. Mater. Textile Eng. **12**(7), 332–339 (2018). https://publications.waset.org/vol/139

12. ElMessiry, M., ElMessiry, A., ElMessiry, M.: Dual token blockchain economy framework. In: International Conference on Blockchain, pp. 157–170. Springer (2019)

13. Kuznetsov, A., Sernani, P., Romeo, L., Frontoni, E., Mancini, A.: On the integration of artificial intelligence and blockchain technology: a perspective about security. IEEE Access (2024)

14. Lee, J.Y.: A decentralized token economy: How blockchain and cryptocurrency can revolutionize business. Bus. Horiz. **62**(6), 773–784 (2019)

15. Lin, I.C., Liao, T.C.: A survey of blockchain security issues and challenges. Int. J. Netw. Secur. **19**(5), 653–659 (2017)

16. Rao, A., Verweij, G.: The impact of artificial intelligence in healthcare: Exploring key legal and ethical challenges. Health Policy Technol. **9**(3), 1–8 (2020)

17. Shifferaw, Y., Lemma, S.: Limitations of proof of stake algorithm in blockchain: a review. Zede J. **39**(1), 81–95 (2021)

18. Zhang, J, et al.: Preventing spread of spam transactions in blockchain by reputation. In: 2020 IEEE/ACM 28th International Symposium on Quality of Service (IWQoS), pp. 1–6. IEEE (2020)
19. Zhao, Y., Yin, D., Wang, L., Yu, Y.: The rise of artificial intelligence, the fall of human wellbeing? Int. J. Soc. Welf. **33**(1), 75–105 (2024)

Application Track

Enhancing Customer Sentiment Analysis: A Hybrid Approach Using VADER and Machine Learning Techniques

Truong Cong Doan[1(✉)], Phan Thanh Duc[2], and Tran Hoang Son[1]

[1] International School, Vietnam National University, Hanoi, Vietnam
{tcdoan,20070977}@vnu.edu.vn
[2] Faculty of Information Technology & Digital Economics, Banking Academy of Vietnam, Hanoi, Vietnam
ducpt@hvnh.edu.vn

Abstract. Analyzing written customer reviews is something every business is focusing on these days. Written customer reviews are a valuable source of information that can provide insights into the system, but dealing with text feedback as unstructured data is difficult. This study utilizes advanced machine learning algorithms and statistics to enhance data quality and analyze customer feedback on Giao Hang Tiet Kiem services. Using a dataset of 12,624 customer evaluations, we applied particular methods such Support Vector Machine (SVM), Logistic Regression, Random Forest, Naive Bayes, and Decision Tree. The Decision Tree algorithm demonstrated the best accuracy at 0.97336 in the first results. Next, by utilising hyperparameter tuning, we were able to enhance the predictive performance and raise accuracy to 0.98205. Afterward, we created a web application that uses Streamlit technology to provide real-time sentiment analysis. This comprehensive approach provides useful insights into improving service quality and customer satisfaction.

Keywords: Customer Feedback · Machine Learning · Decision Tree · Tuning of Hyperparameters · Sentiment Analysis · Data Quality · Giao Hang Tiet Kiem Services

1 Introduction

Information technology has become a core factor thanks to its efficiency, speed and ability to exploit huge amounts of information [1]. To reduce the uncertainty associated with product purchases, users consult reviews and pay attention to online information such as images. According to a research study, most users prioritize customer reviews before purchasing [2]. Faced with that, businesses are shifting from traditional marketing to electronic marketing based on media and social networking platforms, creating a powerful online environment for customers. Collecting and analyzing data from social media has become an important task. Data mining and recommendation technologies are revolutionizing customer feedback analysis, provide insights into their emotions and

X. Pan et al. (Eds.): AIMS 2024, LNCS 15421, pp. 93–102, 2025.
https://doi.org/10.1007/978-3-031-77681-6_7

opinions. AI models such as sentiment analysis and language processing [3]. Natural language helps businesses better understand customers' emotions, opinions and experiences, thereby providing strategies to improve services and increase customer satisfaction. Applying AI in analysis and evaluation not only increases efficiency and accuracy but also helps businesses quickly grasp, respond, and improve customer problems.

Numerous research articles have been published on applying machine learning techniques, particularly decision trees and hyperparameter tuning, to analyze sentiment in customer feedback. The research of Qureshi MA et al. uses algorithms with a high accuracy of 92.25% in classifying sentiment [4]. Similarly, the investigation about the use of BERT embeddings to detect product review helpfulness, resulting in higher accuracy [5]. Another research uses data augmentation to improve sentiment analysis and cross-linguistic understanding [6]. Furthermore, Nayak Sk et all. Uses decision trees and random forests to achieve high disease prediction accuracy [7]. Finally, a research analyzes the non-revisit factor uses sentiment analysis to understand customer dissatisfaction in the tourism industry [8]. These articles frequently use machine learning models such as Decision Trees to analyze customer sentiment, demonstrating AI's potential for processing and understanding feedback. However, they all have limitations, such as suboptimal model accuracy and tuning challenges, and none have been fully integrated into practical web applications. My research fills these gaps by incorporating advanced tuning and deploying a real-time sentiment analysis tool called streamlit, which improves accuracy and usability.

In our article, we use data from CH Play, focusing on the evaluation of Giao Hang Tiet Kiem. The data collection process involves sampling from user to create a rich and diverse data set of customer opinions and sentiments. Algorithms such as Support Vector Machine (SVM), Logistic Regression and Decision Tree have been applied to analyze and classify emotions from these reviews. We also applied Streamlit technology to develop a web application that performs real-time sentiment analysis. The results show that the accuracy of the achieved models is very high, with Decision Tree achieving the highest accuracy. To further improve, we applied the hyperparameter tuning method, which significantly improved the performance of the models. Finally, we successfully built a webapp capable of analyzing and displaying real-time sentiment analysis results, providing key insights to improve service quality and enhance customer's satisfaction.

2 Methodology

2.1 Dataset

The dataset was meticulously taken from CH Play, focusing on user reviews of the Giao Hang Tiet Kiem. It comprises a total of 12,624 records, each representing an individual customer review. The primary attributes include review code, review content, review score, review date, and user-related information such as username and user ID. Each record provides comprehensive details about customer feedback, including the review content, score (on a 5-point scale), and timestamp. This data is crucial for analyzing customer sentiment towards Giao Hang Tiet Kiem services, enabling a deeper understanding of customer perspectives and experiences. Processing and analyzing this data require advanced machine learning techniques and feature extraction methods to ensure accuracy and reliability. In the Table 1, methods such as bag of words and TF-IDF are employed to extract meaningful features from the review content. Additionally, the dataset includes supplementary attributes like frequently occurring keywords and phrases, and user information such as review frequency and sentiment of previous reviews. These attributes provide a nuanced and comprehensive view of customer feedback, facilitating the development of more effective service improvement strategies. The sophisticated analysis underscores the potential for significant insights into customer sentiment and service quality enhancement.

Table 1. Data preprocessing steps and descriptions.

No	Steps	Descriptions
1	Data cleaning	– Remove duplicate reviews and incomplete information – Remove special characters and excessive whitespace
2	Text Preprocessing	– Convert all text to lowercase – Remove unnecessary words – Apply stemming and tokenization techniques
3	Feature Extraction	– Use TF-IDF technique to extract features from the text – Apply Bag of Words to create a feature matrix
4	Kappa	– Use Kappa to check data reliability and ensure consistency between reviews

2.2 Algorithms

In our study, we applied five machine learning algorithms [9, 10] to analyze customer sentiment. We have meticulously applied the method of splitting the dataset and selecting evaluation metrics. The data was split into training and test sets to ensure that the model could adjust and make accurate predictions on new datasets. The primary metric used in our analysis is accuracy to provides a general view of the the model's effectiveness in classifying customer feedback.

Support Vector Machine (SVM)
This particular supervised machine learning approach is used for both regression and classification tasks. It works very well in high-dimensional environments and is commonly used for text classification tasks because of its capacity for handling big feature spaces [11].

Logistic Regression
To model the relationship with a dependent variable, it makes use of a logistic function. It is appropriate for binary and multi-class classification issues since it determines the probability that a given input belongs to a particular class [12].

Decision Tree

This non-parametric supervised learning technique is applied to tasks involving regression and classification. Decision Trees are a popular option for many machine learning applications because of their ease of interpretation and visualization [12].

Random Forest

This machine learning technique uses ensemble learning to control overfitting and increase accuracy by combining forecasts from many trees, making it more robust against data noise [13].

Naive Bayes

Text classification applications like spam identification and sentiment analysis can benefit from this probabilistic classifier since it performs well with high-dimensional data [14].

2.3 Tuning of Hyperparameter

To enhance the effectiveness of machine learning models, hyperparameter optimization was employed. This process involves fine-tuning the settings of a machine learning algorithm to maximize its performance. These parameters could be the quantity of trees in a random forest, the SVM's C parameter value, or other factors that regulate the model's learning process. Tuning techniques such as Grid Search and Random Search were used to find the best parameter combinations for each model [15]. Grid Search explores the entire parameter space by testing all possible combinations, while Random Search selects random combinations of parameters to test, saving time and resources. The results of this tuning process showed that the performance of the models improved significantly, with higher accuracy compared to untuned models.

Research has demonstrated the effectiveness of using hyperparameter tuning methods to enhance the accuracy and performance of models [16]. Specifically, tuning helped us optimize SVM, Logistic Regression, Decision Tree, and Random Forest models, achieving more accurate and reliable sentiment classification results. By employing these tuning methods, we were able to enhance the models' predictive capabilities, ensuring more robust and dependable analysis of customer sentiment.

2.4 Vader

The Sentiment Intensity Analyzer function in Vader Sentiment helps with sentiment computation (Fig. 1). This function creates an analyser for the polarity_scores function in the absence of input. Four values are returned by this method once it receives text: "neg," "neu," "pos," and "com-pound." The values are in the range of -1 to 1, with the 'compound' value being particularly helpful in assessing the degree of sentiment [17]. Analyzing the results of the compound test:

1. Positive sentiment Class: If score is greater than or equal to 0.05
2. Neutral sentiment Class: If score is greater than -0.05 and score is less than 0.05
3. Negative sentiment Class: If score is less than or equal to -0.05

```
# Test the result
sample_review = "This is a good product."
print(vader_analyze_and_label(sample_review))
```

```
({'neg': 0.0, 'neu': 0.58, 'pos': 0.42, 'compound': 0.4404}, 'positive')
```

Fig. 1. Example of testing vader

3 Results

A. Phase 1: Before Tuning

The models were trained and tested on the dataset without any parameter changes prior to applying parameter tweaking. The accompanying bar chart, which attempts to show the accuracy of each model in identifying the data, shows the outcomes of these models. Models such as were applied and evaluated based on their prediction performance.

The data was first split into two sets: the testing set and the training set. The TF-IDF method was used to preprocess this data and turn it into numerical features [18]. Subsequently, the models were trained on the training set and tested on the test set. Accuracy was the main performance criterion utilised to assess the models. The results illustrate that the Decision Tree reached the highest accuracy with 0.973360, while Naive Bayes had the lowest accuracy with 0.733996. These results (Fig. 2) were compiled and presented in a bar chart, providing a visual comparison of the performance across the models.

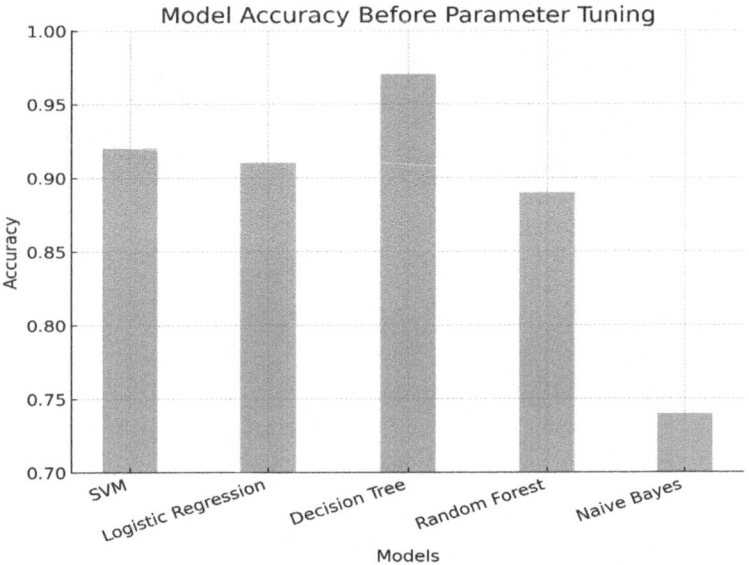

Fig. 2. A figure shows the model accuracy of 5 algorithms before parameter tuning

B. Phase 2: After Tuning

After applying parameter tuning, the performance of most machine learning models has been significantly improved. Parameter tuning is performed through techniques such as Grid Search to search for optimal parameter values, in order to enhance the classification ability of the model [19]. The results after parameter tuning show that the highest model after tuning has better results than the highest model before tuning, demonstrating the effectiveness of the optimization method.

Specifically, after tuning, the SVM model achieved an accuracy increase of 0.960636, while the Decision Tree achieved 0.986083, the highest level among the tested models. In contrast, the Logistic Regression after tuning slightly decreased in accuracy to 0.827435. The results (Fig. 3) of the best model after tuning are presented in a bar graph, allowing for a visual comparison of the change in performance before and after tuning.

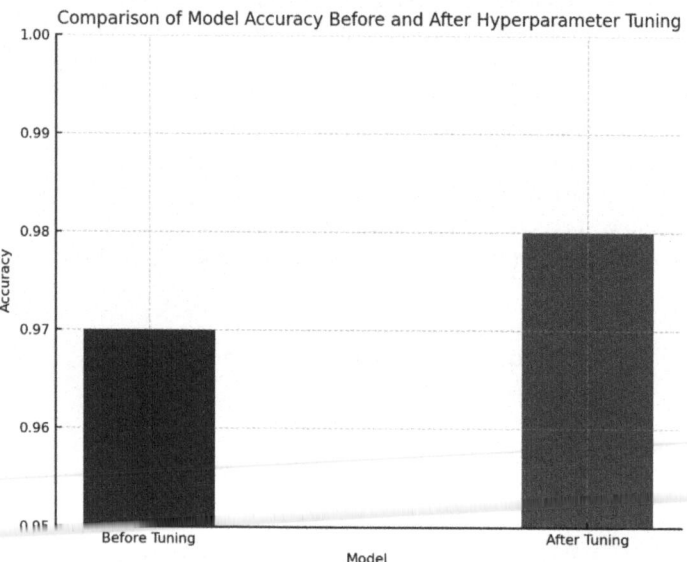

Fig. 3. A figure shows the comparison of accuracy between the best model before tuning and after tuning

C. Phase 3: Web Technology Introduction

In this study, we used Streamlit technology to develop a real-time sentiment analysis web application for Giao Hang Tiet Kiem. It is a modern and powerful framework designed to create interactive web applications in Python quickly and efficiently. Research has demonstrated the effectiveness of Streamlit in various applications, highlighting its potential in simplifying the deployment of data-driven applications [20]. Specifically, we used this to build a web application that allows real-time sentiment analysis of customer feedback, providing detailed and useful information to improve service quality. The features of it enabled us to easily deploy complex machine learning models and create interactive dashboards, supporting the data-driven decision-making process.

VADER Sentiment Analysis

Enter your review:

> good delivery

Sentiment: **Positive**

Scores: {'neg': 0.0, 'neu': 0.256, 'pos': 0.744, 'compound': 0.4404}

Decision Tree Classification Report

Decision Tree Results after Hyperparameter Tuning

	Class	Precision	Recall	F1-Score	Support
0	negative	0.9415	1	0.9699	306
1	neutral	0.9882	0.9949	0.9916	1,181
2	positive	0.998	0.9718	0.9847	1,028
3	accuracy	0.9861	0.9861	0.9861	2,515
4	macro avg	0.9759	0.9889	0.9821	2,515
5	weighted avg	0.9865	0.9861	0.9861	2,515

Fig. 4. A figure shows the application's interface on streamlit

Streamlit, an open-source platform, facilitates the creation of dynamic web applications directly from Python scripts. For the development of our WebApp (Fig. 4), Streamlit was selected for its user-friendly nature and robust Python integration, enabling swift transformation of data analysis models into dynamic web apps. We incorporated the Valence Aware Dictionary and Sentiment Reasoner (Vader) for sentiment analysis tasks. The outcomes of this analysis and the performance evaluations of the optimized machine learning models, which featured measures such as accuracy, recall, and F1-Score, were displayed through Streamlit's capabilities.

4 Conclusion

In the word cloud of positive reviews (Fig. 5), prominent keywords include "customer," "order," "app," "good," "delivery," and "service. "This indicates that customers are satisfied with their interactions with Giao Hang Tiet Kiem's services, particularly with the mobile app and the order process. The frequent mention of "delivery" also suggests that customers appreciate Giao Hang Tiet Kiem's delivery service.

In the word cloud of negative reviews (Fig. 6), the words "bad," "order," "delivery," and "error" stand out significantly. This suggests that Giao Hang Tiet Kiem lacks consistency in handling orders, as some customers are pleased with the delivery service while others are not. Additionally, errors occurring during the ordering process, possibly during peak hours when many users are logged in simultaneously, indicate that Giao Hang Tiet Kiem needs to improve the quality of their application. Moreover, "money" is also a factor mentioned here, indicating that customers might be dissatisfied with the

Positive Reviews

Fig. 5. Cloudword of Positive Reviews

costs associated with Giao Hang Tiet Kiem's services. These complaints may relate to delivery fees, hidden costs, or a perceived mismatch between the price paid and the quality of service received. To address this, Giao Hang Tiet Kiem should review its pricing structure to ensure competitiveness and greater transparency regarding costs. Offering additional promotions or flexible service packages could also help alleviate customer dissatisfaction related to financial aspects.

Negative Reviews

Fig. 6. Cloudword of Negative Reviews

In this research, we applied machine learning methods to analyze customer feedback data to assess their sentiments towards Giao Hang Tiet Kiem's delivery service. We experimented with different models, followed by parameter tuning to innovative the performance of these models. The results after tuning showed a significant increase in the accuracy of the models, particularly with the Decision Tree.

Looking forward, we plan to expand this research by applying additional natural language processing techniques to enhance sentiment analysis capabilities, as well as integrating deep learning models to further improve accuracy and the ability to handle complex data.

References

1. Varey, R.: Internal marketing: a review and some interdisciplinary research challenges. Int. J. Serv. Ind. Manag. **6**, 40–63 (1995). https://doi.org/10.1108/09564239510078849
2. The impact of work life balance on employee attitudes and behavior in health care sector. https://repository.effatuniversity.edu.sa/handle/20.500.14131/1417. Accessed 30 Aug 2024
3. Ishtiaq, A., Munir, K., Raza, A., Abdelsamee, N., Jamjoom, M., Ullah, Z.: Product helpfulness detection with novel transformer based BERT embedding and class probability features. IEEE Access. (2024). https://doi.org/10.1109/ACCESS.2024.3390605
4. Qureshi, M.A., et al.: Sentiment analysis of reviews in natural language: Roman Urdu as a case study. IEEE Access **10**, 24945–24954 (2022). https://doi.org/10.1109/ACCESS.2022.3150172
5. Ishtiaq, A., Munir, K., Raza, A., Samee, N.A., Jamjoom, M.M., Ullah, Z.: Product helpfulness detection with novel transformer based BERT embedding and class probability features. IEEE Access **12**, 55905–55917 (2024). https://doi.org/10.1109/ACCESS.2024.3390605
6. Tareq, M., Islam, M., Deb, S., Rahman, S., Mahmud, A.A.: Data-augmentation for Bangla-English code-mixed sentiment analysis: enhancing cross linguistic contextual understanding. IEEE Access **11**, 51657–51671 (2023). https://doi.org/10.1109/ACCESS.2023.3277787
7. Nayak, S.K., Garanayak, M., Swain, S.K., Panda, S.K., Godavarthi, D.: An intelligent disease prediction and drug recommendation prototype by using multiple approaches of machine learning algorithms. IEEE Access **11**, 99304–99318 (2023). https://doi.org/10.1109/ACCESS.2023.3314332
8. Chang, J.-R., Chen, M.-Y., Chen, L.-S., Tseng, S.-C.: Why customers don't revisit in tourism and hospitality industry? IEEE Access **7**, 146588–146606 (2019). https://doi.org/10.1109/ACCESS.2019.2946168
9. Truong, C.D., Nguyen, V.C., Kim Oanh, N.T.: Estimating smartphone price ranges using machine learning models. In: Nguyen, T.D.L., Dawson, M., Ngoc, L.A., and Lam, K.Y. (eds.) Proceedings of the International Conference on Intelligent Systems and Networks. ICISN 2024. Lecture Notes in Networks and Systems, vol. 1077, pp. 697–707. Springer, Singapore (2024). https://doi.org/10.1007/978-981-97-5504-2_80
10. Truong, C.D., Tran, D.Q., Nguyen, V.D., Tran, H.T., Hoang, T.D.: Predicting vietnamese stock market using the variants of LSTM architecture. In: Cong Vinh, P., Huu Nhan, N. (eds.) Nature of Computation and Communication. ICTCC 2021. Lecture Notes of the Institute for Computer Sciences, Social Informatics and Telecommunications Engineering, vol. 408, pp. 129–137. Springer, Cham (2021). https://doi.org/10.1007/978-3-030-92942-8_11
11. Cortes, C., Vapnik, V.: Support-vector networks. Mach. Learn. **20**, 273–297 (1995). https://doi.org/10.1007/BF00994018
12. Hosmer, D.W., Lemeshow, S., Sturdivant, R.X.: Applied Logistic Regression. Wiley (2013). https://doi.org/10.1002/9781118548387
13. Devyatkin, D.A., Grigoriev, O.G.: Random kernel forests. IEEE Access **10**, 77962–77979 (2022). https://doi.org/10.1109/ACCESS.2022.3193385
14. Rish, I.: An empirical study of the Naïve Bayes classifier. In: IJCAI 2001 Workshop on Empirical Methods in Artificial Intelligence, vol. 3 (2001)
15. Liashchynskyi, P., Liashchynskyi, P.: Grid search, random search, genetic algorithm: a big comparison for NAS. (2019)
16. Bergstra, J., Bergstra, J., Bengio, Y., Bengio, Y.: Random search for hyper-parameter optimization
17. Mahmoudi, A., Jemielniak, D., Ciechanowski, L.: Assessing accuracy: a study of lexicon and rule-based packages in R and python for sentiment analysis. IEEE Access **12**, 20169–20180 (2024). https://doi.org/10.1109/ACCESS.2024.3353692

18. Ahuja, R., Chug, A., Kohli, S., Gupta, S., Ahuja, P.: The impact of features extraction on the sentiment analysis. Procedia Comput. Sci. **152**, 341–348 (2019). https://doi.org/10.1016/j.procs.2019.05.008
19. Rehan, M., Malik, M.S.I., Jamjoom, M.M.: Fine-tuning transformer models using transfer learning for multilingual threatening text identification. IEEE Access **11**, 106503–106515 (2023). https://doi.org/10.1109/ACCESS.2023.3320062
20. Patil, S., Lokesha, V.: Live Twitter sentiment analysis using streamlit framework. SSRN Electron. J. (2022). https://doi.org/10.2139/ssrn.4119949

Short Paper Track

Flood Inundation Range Prediction Method Based on SRR-Informer

Han Liu$^{(\boxtimes)}$ ⓘ, Zhihao Chen ⓘ, and Qi Sun ⓘ

College of Computer Science and Software Engineering, Hohai University, Nanjing, China
221307050003@hhu.edu.cn

Abstract. Flood forecasting methods based on deep learning rely on a large number of observational data, and are facing serious challenges in areas with scarce data. Aiming at the problems of flood inundated range prediction in areas with scarce data, this paper proposes a flood inundated range prediction method based on spatial reduction reconstruction (SRR) and improved deep attention neural network (Informer) to reduce the data requirements of the two core parts of water level simulation and spatial modeling. It alleviates the problem of insufficient observational data for flood inundation range prediction in areas with scarce data. This method obtains the dependency relationship of long time series data through Informer model, and inserts the built-in input selection layer to reduce the number of parameters in the model, reducing the data requirement of water level simulation. At the same time, the SRR algorithm is used to select the representative locations that are easy to be inundated in the basin, which reduces the number of locations required for spatial modeling of flood inundation range and the corresponding data requirements. The experimental results show that this method can improve the accuracy of flood inundation range prediction and speed up the efficiency of the model.

Keywords: Deep learning · Data scarcity · Flood inundation range forecast

1 Introduction

Globally, about 75 million people are affected and more than 20,000 people die from floods every year [1]. Flood inundation range prediction is mainly based on flow prediction, hydrological model and topographic map data, but it is difficult to obtain accurate forecasts for most flood-hit areas due to the lack of complete and accurate hydrological observations, i.e., data scarcity [2]. At present, the prediction of flood inundation range is mainly based on traditional hydrodynamic models. Teng et al. [3] proposed a simple one-dimensional model according to the complexity of the river-flood inundation area network, while Liu et al. [4] proposed a more complex two-dimensional model and a two-dimensional mixed model. Some scholars have also studied flood range prediction methods based on deep learning models to achieve faster and more reliable flood inundation modeling. Tamiru and Wagari [5] integrated deep learning with HEC-RAS into a hydraulic model. Kabir et al. [6] studied the application of CNN model in predicting the

© The Author(s), under exclusive license to Springer Nature Switzerland AG 2025
X. Pan et al. (Eds.): AIMS 2024, LNCS 15421, pp. 105–112, 2025.
https://doi.org/10.1007/978-3-031-77681-6_8

inundated range of flash floods. Zhou et al. [7] used long-term memory networks and spatial reduction models to model time series in flood inundated data and reduce information redundancy. General deep learning models cannot accurately grasp the dependency between long time series flow data and water level data in hydrological simulation tasks, which increases the unnecessary data requirements for water level simulation. In addition, inundation range prediction usually requires a complete modeling of the entire region, complex modeling also leads to low forecasting efficiency and makes it difficult to meet the real-time demand of flood forecasting system [8].

Based on this, this paper proposes a flood inundation range prediction method based on spatial reduction reconstruction and improved deep attention neural network, called SRR-Informer model, which mainly includes two important operations: water level simulation module and spatial simplification module. Among them, the structure of the water level simulation module (Informer model) can effectively obtain the dependence relationship of long time series data (runoff – water level), so as to simulate the water level with less data. The spatial reduction and reconstruction (SRR) algorithm of the spatial simplification module selects the representative location in the modeling domain, and reduces the modeling location and the corresponding data amount required for the prediction of the inundation range.

2 Flood Inundation Range Prediction Method Based on SRR-Informer

2.1 Water Level Simulation Method Based on Informer

Informer model [9] is a new and improved structure of deep attention neural network model (Transformer) for long time series data features. Based on Transformer model, Informer structure introduces knowledge distillation operation and ProbSparse self-attention mechanism to reduce the complexity of the original self-attention module. In this paper, a multi-layer Informer encoder modified according to the above process is used to learn the long time series data, and finally, a unique generative decoder designed by Informer is used to handle the mapping relationship from flow to water level.

Training Process
The input data for the Informer model is normalized using the following functions:

$$x' = (x_i - x_{min})/(x_{max} - x_{min}) \tag{1}$$

where x_i is the observed value, and x_{max} and x_{min} are the maximum and minimum values of the flow prediction, respectively.

The Informer model requires the previous time series as input variables, $X = (x_t, x_{t+1}, \ldots, x_{t+w-1})$, where x_t is the daily input feature for day t and $|X| = w$ is the window size. The goal of the model is to predict the next time step water level in the data scarce area:

$$y_{t+w}^D = Informer(X = (x_t, x_{t+1}, \ldots, x_{t+w-1})) \tag{2}$$

Data X is first entered into the knowledge distillation layer. In this layer, the t-th sequence input X^t is first shaped into a matrix $X_{en}^t \in \mathbb{R}^{L_x \times d_{model}}$. The specific "distillation" process is shown as follows:

$$X_{j+1}^t = \text{MaxPool}(\text{ELU}(\text{Conv}1d([X_j^t]_{AB}))) \tag{3}$$

where $[\cdot]_{AB}$ represents the attention block, $Conv1d(\cdot)$ uses the $ELU(\cdot)$ activation function to perform a one-dimensional convolution filter (kernel width $= 3$) in the time dimension, adding a maximum pool layer with step size 2.

The position is then embedded into the input feature added to the distillation to obtain the first layer of input characterization H_t^0:

$$H_t^0 = x_t + E_{p_t} \tag{4}$$

where the superscript 0 represents the indicator layer index, and the subscript t is the time state. E_p is a positional embedding obtained by a positional coding formula. After obtaining the input representations H^0, input them into several Transformer layers and feature representation learning is carried out according to the following formula:

$$H_t^1 = \text{LN}(\text{FFN}(H_t^1) + H_t^1) \tag{5}$$

$$H_t^1 = \text{LN}(\mathcal{A}(Q_t^0, K^0, V^0) + H_t^0) \tag{6}$$

$$\mathcal{A}(Q, K, V) = \text{Softmax}\left(\frac{\overline{Q}K^\top}{\sqrt{d}}\right)V \tag{7}$$

$$Q^0 = H^0 W^Q \tag{8}$$

$$K^0, V^0 = H^0 W^K, H^0 W^V \tag{9}$$

where $\mathcal{A}$ is a probabilistic sparse self-attention mechanism, $\overline{Q}$ is a sparse matrix of the same size as q,and it contains only Top-u queries under the sparsity metric M (q, K); LN is a layer normalization operation, and FFN represents a fully connected feed-forward layer. The intermediate state is then obtained after calculation at the $L\times$ encoder layer.

Use a standard decoder structure for water level prediction. However, generative reasoning can be used to mitigate speed dips in long predictions, providing the following vectors to the decoder:

$$X_{de}^t = \text{Concat}(X_{token}^t, X_0^t) \in \mathbb{R}^{(L_{token}+L_y) \times d_{model}} \tag{10}$$

where $X_{token}^t \in \mathbb{R}^{L_{token} \times d_{model}}$ is the starting sequence of the traffic at the target location, and $X_0^t \in \mathbb{R}^{L_y \times d_{model}}$ is the ending sequence of the traffic at the target location (set the scalar to 0).

The final output representation vector $H^L \in R^{w \times d}$ is obtained after the calculation of the generative decoder, where w is the input sequence length (window size) and d is the vector dimension.

For water level prediction, another layer can be added to project the representation vector H^I into the real environment:

$$y_{t+w}^D = H_{t+w-1}^L W^y + b^y \tag{11}$$

where $W^y \in R^{d \times 4}$ and $b^y \in R^4$.

Built-in Input Selection Layer

This paper designs a built-in input selection (BIIS) layer and uses the Information inheritance rate (*IFR*) to quantify the importance of each input variable entered into the BIIS layer.

Informer Water Level Simulation Model with BIIS

The Informer model architecture with a built-in input selection layer is shown in Fig. 1.

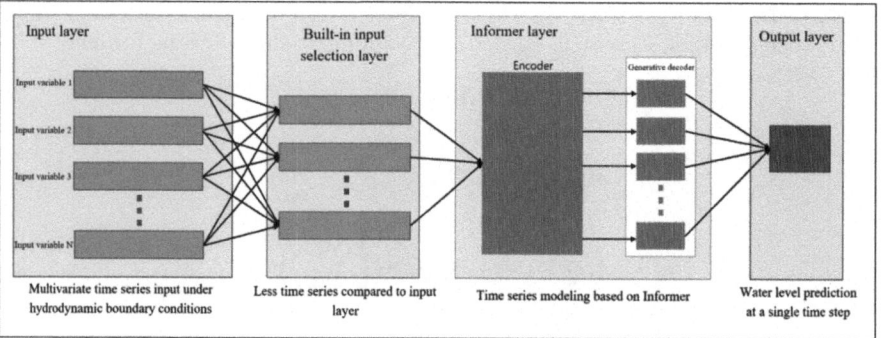

Fig. 1. Overview of Informer water level simulation model with BIIS

2.2 Spatial Reduction Reconstruction Algorithm

In this section, a spatial reduction reconstruction algorithm (SRR) is proposed. It is mainly composed of three main algorithms: representative location selection algorithm (SRR-RL), inundated range reconstruction algorithm (SRR-RECO) and drainage path search algorithm (SRR-search).

The drainage path search algorithm (SRR-Search) is designed to search the drainage path from each given starting point, whose starting position is determined by the range of inundation.

The representative location selection algorithm (SRR-RL) is designed to reduce the number of locations required for Informer modeling and focus its modeling on data-rich regions. The SRR-RL is designed to find a key location in the model domain where the water level is modeled and later called the representative location (RL).

The inundation range reconstruction algorithm (SRR-Reco) is used to reconstruct the inundation range according to the water level at RL. It uses 2D linear interpolation method to reconstruct the inundation range according to the simulated water level at the RL and the model boundary. Then, the range of interpolation is compared with the digital elevation model (DEM) of the region, and the region where the water level is lower than the elevation is eliminated to adjust the range. Finally, the adjusted range is saved in geo-tiff format as the output of the SRR-Reco module.

3   Experiments

3.1   Experimental Data and Evaluation Metrics

CAMELS dataset was derived from the United States Geological Survey, based on the comprehensive hydrological data set of 671 River Basin observation points recorded by USGS, this paper selected 41 river basin observation points in 030202 observation stations cluster (Neuse River Basin) CAMELS data set as research objects. Since 2000, 11 observation points in this basin cluster have been lacking in observation data of discharge for a long time, and two observation points have obvious adjacent basins (upstream and downstream basins), so they are selected as data scarce areas to carry out the main research. Meanwhile, the paper also obtains the digital elevation map (DEM) data of the Hydrological data and maps made by USGS for spatial modeling. The spatial resolution of DEM data is 30 s.

In this paper, probability of detection (POD) and false alarm rate (RFA) are commonly used to evaluate the maximum inundate range of flood.

3.2   Verify the Effect of Flood Inundation Range Prediction Method Based on SRR-Informer

Experimental Scheme
Evaluate the effectiveness of the inundation range prediction method based on SRR-Informer, and study the accuracy and efficiency of the method respectively. Data sets are divided as shown in Table 1.

Table 1. Dataset partition

Dataset type	Year	Time interval	Site number	Event number
Training set	1981~1990	Day	41	27
Validation set	1991~2000	Hour	33	14
Test set	2001~2010	Hour	28	11

Reference Model

In this section of experiments, the accurate comparison of submerged range prediction methods based on deep learning is mainly discussed. The specific comparison algorithm is shown as follows:

CNN: Convolutional neural networks.
GAN: Generative adversarial network.
RNN: Recurrent neural network.

Details of Experimental Parameters

Parameters of the SRR-Informer modeling method are as follows: The batch epoch is 40, the drop rate is 0.2, the learning rate is 0.0005, the batch_size is 200, and the sequence length is 48. The optimizers are Adam and mean square error (MSE).

Evaluation of Flood Inundation Range Prediction Accuracy

In order to distinguish the performance of different models in the task of flood inundation modeling range prediction, this section first visualized the prediction of the maximum inundation range of the flood event in this region at 21:00 on September 19, 2018, and initially analyzed the prediction results of different models in the flood inundation range.

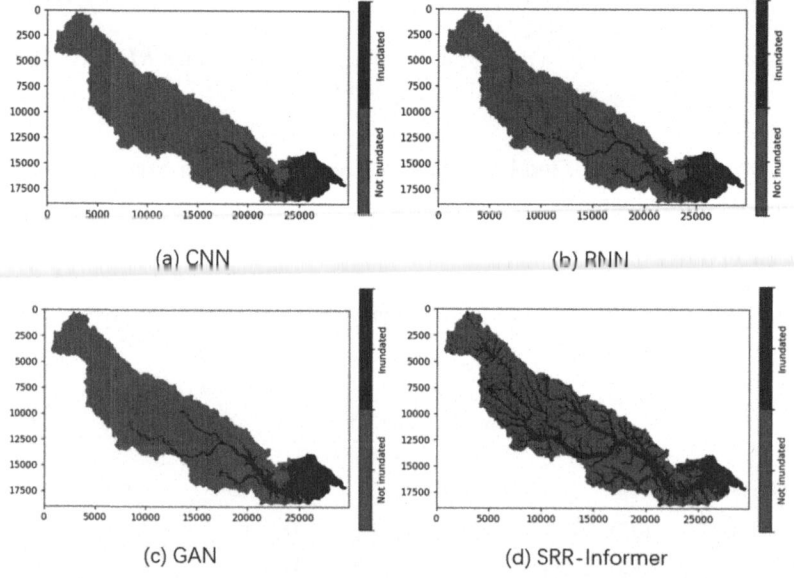

Fig. 2. Prediction of maximum range of flood inundation by different models

Among Fig. 2, the prediction range of the maximum inundation range by the SRR-Informer modeling method is the largest. Then, combined with the actual maximum inundation range in flood events, the accuracy of SRR-Informer flood range prediction is analyzed in detail.

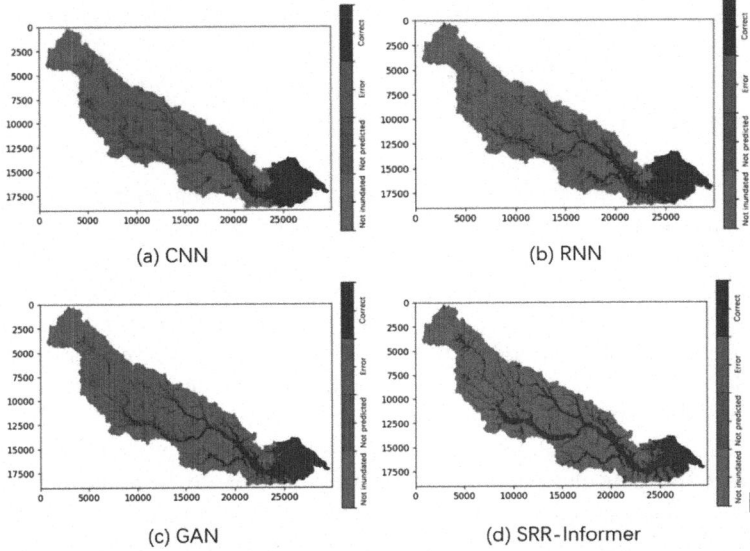

Fig. 3. Comparison of prediction performance of inundation range combined with real events (Color figure online)

The blue part in Fig. 3 represents the accurate prediction part. The green part represents the missing part of the forecast. The red part represents the part of the prediction error. In general, the prediction error probability of SRR-Informer modeling method is low.

POD and *RFA* were also selected as evaluation indicators in this section to evaluate the model's performance, as shown in Table 2.

Table 2. Compared with the accuracy of the maximum flood inundation range simulated by the reference model

Model	*POD*	*RFA*
MLP	43.6%	5.9%
CNN	52.9%	7.2%
RNN	74.1%	6.4%
GAN	70.7%	6.9%
SRR-Informer	94.2%	4.8%

In the probability of detection (*POD*), the modeling effect of SRR-Informer method is far superior to other deep learning methods, and the accuracy is close to 95%. SRR-Informer also outperforms other models in the false Alarm rate metric (*RFA*). The above experiments prove that the SRR-Informer modeling method can mine the time series data of historical flood events, so as to obtain more accurate flood inundation range in areas with scarce data.

4 Conclusion

Aiming at the problem that the high data demand of the inundation range prediction model cannot be met in the data scarce area, this paper proposes the inundation range prediction method based on SRR-Informer to reduce the data demand of the two parts of water level simulation and spatial modeling. Firstly, the dependence relationship of long time series data is obtained by Informer model, and the number of parameters required by the model is reduced by adding the built-in input selection layer to the model, so as to reduce the amount of data required for water level simulation. Secondly, SRR algorithm is applied to select the representative locations in the model domain, which reduces the number of locations required for spatial modeling of the inundation range and the corresponding amount of data. The results are close to the actual range, and the operating efficiency is higher than other reference models. Although this paper mainly focuses on flood inundation range prediction as the research orientation, its essence is to study the problem definition and modeling method oriented to data scarcity. Its practical application is not limited to the field of water conservancy, and it will also have certain reference significance for other fields.

References

1. Sanyal, J.: Flood inundation modelling in data-sparse flatlands: challenges and prospects. In: Floods in the Ganga–Brahmaputra–Meghna Delta, pp. 9–35 (2023)
2. Momoi, M., Kotsuki, S., Kikuchi, R., et al.: Emulating rainfall-runoff-inundation model using deep neural network with dimensionality reduction. Artif. Intell. Earth Syst., 1–25 (2023)
3. Teng, J., Jakeman, A.J., Vaze, J., et al.: Flood inundation modelling: a review of methods recent advances and uncertainty analysis. Environ Model Softw. **90**, 201–216 (2017)
4. Liu, Q., Qin, Y., Zhang, Y., et al.: A coupled 1D–2D hydrodynamic model for flood simulation in flood detention basin. Nat. Hazards **75**, 1303–1325 (2015)
5. Tamiru, H., Wagari, M.: Machine-learning and HEC-RAS integrated models for flood inundation mapping in Baro River Basin. Ethiopia. Model. Earth Syst. Environ. **8**(2), 2291–2303 (2022)
6. Kabir, S., Patidar, S., Xia, X., et al.: A deep convolutional neural network model for rapid prediction of fluvial flood inundation. J. Hydrol. **590**, 125481 (2020)
7. Zhou, Y., Wu, W., Nathan, R., et al.: A rapid flood inundation modelling framework using deep learning with spatial reduction and reconstruction. Environ Model Softw. **143**, 105112 (2021)
8. Wu, W., Emerton, R., Duan, Q., et al.: Ensemble flood forecasting: current status and future opportunities. Wiley Interdiscip. Rev. Water **7**(3), e1432 (2020)
9. Zhou, H., Zhang, S., Peng, J., et al.: Informer: beyond efficient transformer for long sequence time-series forecasting. In: Proceedings of the AAAI Conference on Artificial Intelligence, vol. 35(12), pp. 11106–11115 (2021)

Author Index